30 Second Seduction

HOW ADVERTISERS LURE WOMEN THROUGH FLATTERY, FLIRTATION, AND MANIPULATION

Andrea Gardner

D1264087

SEAL PRESS

30-Second Seduction
HOW ADVERTISERS LURE WOMEN THROUGH
FLATTERY, FLIRTATION, AND MANIPULATION

Copyright © 2008 by Andrea Gardner

Published by
Seal Press
A Member of the Perseus Books Group
1700 Fourth Street
Berkeley, CA 94710

Library of Congress Cataloging-in-Publication Data

Gardner, Andrea.
30-second seduction: how advertisers lure women through flattery, flirtation, and manipulation/by Andrea Gardner.
p. cm.
"An Imprint of Avalon Publishing Group."
ISBN-13: 978-1-58005-212-2
ISBN-10: 1-58005-212-6
1. Women consumers—United States. 2. Women in advertising—United States. 3. Marketing—United States. I. Title. II. Title: Thirty second seduction.

HF5415.33.U6G34 2008
659.101'9—dc22
2007039236

Cover design by Susan Koski Zucker
Interior design by Domini Dragoone
Printed in the United States of America
Distributed by Publishers Group West

For Nick

Contents

Introduction

From the time we wake up in the morning until we return to sleep at night, we encounter thousands of marketing messages. They begin with commercials for orange juice and eggs on morning news programs. As we drive to work, we see ads for banks, computers, and cars plastered onto billboards. We see logos on food packaging, T-shirts, and cars. Pop-up ads for shoes, pet food, and retail stores greet us when we log on to our email. Commercials for Coke usher in movies at the theater. Ads for cosmetics, Botox, and perfume lie side by side in magazines and newspapers.

Advertisements are inescapable and growing by the year.

Experts say the average person encounters up to five thousand ad messages each day, yet until I began covering the advertising industry as a reporter, I didn't think much about the motivation behind those messages, or how those messages impacted what I wanted, what I bought, what I thought was normal, and what I wanted my life to look and feel like.

Over the course of my life, commercials have made their mark. It started at the age of five, when I developed a strong connection with Mrs. Butterworth. Each time I sat at the kitchen table, waiting for pancakes, I would stare up at Mrs. Butterworth, hoping she would speak to me the same way she would in the popular commercial. It was the first time I experienced the power of advertising. Pinnacle Foods, the company that made Mrs. Butterworth, had me hooked. They had gotten their girl.

From that point on, I was won over. I begged my mom for the Barbie dream house. I wondered why my parents didn't have breakfast in bed every morning, like in the Folgers coffee commercial. In junior high school I used Noxzema, so that my skin would be as clear and glowing as Rebecca Gayheart's. In high school, I saw an ad that featured a college girl living in a dorm room. Three years later, when I moved into *my* first dorm, I was disappointed that my room was so small and dingy. I longed to eventually wear a beautiful business suit and prance across a New York City street, like the woman in that Finesse shampoo ad did . . . or was it Prell? Oh, to be shower clean with a great job in the big city. At twenty-five, I loved the VW commercial where two friends spot an abandoned couch on the sidewalk and take it home, where it fits perfectly in their hip studio loft (sigh). One day, my couch would come.

Through my work as a journalist, I have come to understand the building blocks of the ad and marketing worlds. Marketing encompasses all of the actions a company takes to bring buyers to its products. Advertising is one part of marketing, and it comes in the form of messages that a company pays to put into the public domain via the media. In learning about the business, I've realized that advertising and marketing professionals are, at the most basic level, good flirts. Their techniques are similar to the tactics boys in high school use to win the affection of the girls. Back in school, smart Romeos did their research, surprising my friends and me with mix tapes of our favorite songs. Other guys played the class clown. The persistent ones bombarded us with notes and phone calls. Still others tried the "just friends" method, commiserating with us about chemistry and taking the bus. Advertisers do the same thing. They pass us notes as we check our email, whisper sweet nothings to us through the radio, crash the party through product placement during our favorite television shows, and endear themselves to us through commercials that make us giggle.

Fortune 500 companies and marketing firms are as ambitious and driven as a teenage boy, though some can be just as clueless. Many either avoided or misunderstood women for decades, and some are still struggling with comprehending them. The ones that are seducing us have made their sales pitches relevant by doing their homework. They take their cues from trends in popular culture and social research, which tell them who we women are, what we want, and how society and media are shaping our sensibilities. Not all of their flirtation techniques work on everyone, but each technique is meant for someone.

Over the past two years, I've interviewed a slew of professionals from the marketing field—consultants who specialize in marketing to women, executives from some of the top corporations in America, and professionals from advertising firms. Many of them openly explained their approach to reaching women. I also spoke to everyday women about how they experience the barrage of corporate America's advances. I found these women a number of ways. Many were referred to me by friends and family. Some I found after reading their blog or MySpace page. Some of the women are friends and acquaintances of mine from college, or former coworkers.

These candid, thoughtful ladies told me about the brands that won them over, commercials that made them laugh, messages they couldn't ignore, and ad campaigns that just felt fake. They hail from various parts of the United States and Canada, come from different socioeconomic and educational backgrounds, and are different ethnicities and ages. I worked hard to get a diverse mix. We talked about their daily lives: their relationships, their lifestyles, and their identities. They told me how their sensibilities have changed over time, and how brands have recognized that by incorporating societal shifts into their ads. Many of these women described their daily dose of advertising as a bombardment they couldn't escape—an annoying static that buzzes around them all day, though most women know very little about the driving forces behind those messages.

I have written this book to help you connect the dots. You'll explore the well-oiled inner workings of the marketing world and discover the art, science, and business used to seduce you. All along the way, you'll learn more about today's women, and how social changes, pop culture trends, life-stage events, and generational distinctions define them.

I also hope this book empowers your future purchases. For many years, women's advocates, feminists, and some marketing consultants have tried to influence companies to drop the sex-laden, objectifying, unattainable, stereotypical images in advertising. But, apart from a few exceptions, companies have been resistant to change. Certainly there are glimmers of hope, and these are discussed in the following chapters. However, there is considerable room for improvement. Most advertising today could be more empowering, entertaining, and realistic.

Consumers need to demand it. Women in particular have the consumer power to influence Madison Avenue to step up its game. After all, we make about 80 percent of the buying decisions in America. Companies know this—that's why they are flirting their way into our wallets. In order for advertising to drastically improve, women need to stop tuning out ads and should begin to judge companies on their advertising and marketing advances. The companies that court them properly should win their business. Our dollars can dictate how advertisers speak to us in the future. Our awareness and action could result in ads that are bursting with relevant messages, inspiring stories, hilarious punch lines, and realistic-looking women. We can't escape the bombardment that comes from Madison Avenue, but we women have the power to force big businesses to improve the way they speak to us every day.

CHAPTER 1

The Scholar

The scholar on campus always does his homework. And when he falls for a girl, he immediately puts on his thinking cap, learning as much as he can about his prospective girlfriend.

Fortune 500 companies and marketing firms are no different. Having finally woken up to the fact that women make approximately 80 percent of household buying decisions, marketing professionals are now in a dash to learn as much as they can about women. They realize that female consumers aren't just buying the Tupperware, laundry detergent, and groceries. Women more often choose the family home, healthcare plan, bank, car, computer, and vacation destination. While men still make more money than women, the lady of the house will most often decide what to do with the household's money, regardless of whether it comes from her own paycheck or her partner's.

In an interview I conducted with women's marketing expert and author Marti Barletta in January 2007, she said that until the start of the new millennium, many businesspeople didn't realize or accept that women make the majority of household buying decisions, including the big-ticket items. When she first began public-speaking engagements based on her groundbreaking book *Marketing to Women,* she had to convince attendees that women had money in the first place. Barletta said this false perception that women don't have their own money is due in part to the news media, which ran what she calls "the poor story," contending that women make less money than men and are often held back from achieving top management positions at work. While that is factual, people were led to believe that women hold less buying power, when in fact women are the chief spenders of their households. Business and marketing folks also assumed that men made the big buying decisions, because men statistically are "early adopters," flocking to new technological products before women do. What many didn't realize, Barletta said, is that once an item goes mainstream, women gain interest and become the principal buyers.

Women's marketing consultant and author Lisa Johnson told me that when marketers started trying to attract female buyers, their thinking was too simple and stereotypical. Many assumed that women would buy a new version of a product if it came in the color pink. Some banks even painted their interior walls pink. Other companies chose not to market to female consumers at all, because they were fearful that feminizing their brands would alienate their male customers. For many, marketing to women was a risk that wasn't worth taking.

Barletta said that more than laziness or resistance, there was a lack of knowledge in the industry. "It was more a matter that nobody knew. People didn't realize . . . that women would buy differently [from] men. There have been huge changes over the last thirty years." Among those changes is the dramatic impact that research has had on the marketing industry. Marketers and corporate folks have been turned into scholars, well schooled on the power of female consumers, as well as on how women think, shop, and interpret messages in advertising. In the last ten years, Barletta explained, we've seen scientific research on brain anatomy, bio-chemistry, the hormones that govern different behaviors, and how com-munication differs between the sexes. The data is coupled with other kinds of research, such as studies and surveys that explain social, cultural, and generational differences among women.

Barletta, Johnson, and other researchers and consultants make up a grow-ing field within the marketing world. What started as a handful of research firms has grown into thousands of consultancies. Many are devoted solely to studying women. Of those companies, some study only the habits and sensi-bilities of moms. Others concentrate solely on women under thirty, or women over fifty. There are researchers for seemingly every subgroup of consumer, and there is a wide variety of research studies. Some go the route of asking women to fill out surveys. Others do ethnographic research, where marketers go into the homes of consumers and watch them in their natural habitats. Other times, marketers recruit a group of women who then serve as a consulting board for brands as they develop products and marketing campaigns.

Some researchers place sensors on consumers' heads and monitor how brain activity changes as consumers watch ads. Others use MRI technology to achieve the same goal. In the ad world, this kind of research is known as neuromarketing. Many in the industry question whether neuromarketing can efficiently detect consumer behavior, though neuromarketing advocates point out that traditional focus group and survey research is also plagued with inconsistency problems. Many in the industry believe that consumers aren't completely honest when they are simply asked their opinions, because they fear the judgment of the surveyor or other consumers in the focus group session. Other researchers believe consumer feedback withers in the sterile focus-group environment because it is so removed from the normal consumer experience.

Jet Blue tried to overcome that problem. In one research study, the company created a booth that looked just like an airplane's cabin. Passersby were invited to sit in a seat, pull the tray table down, and recall memories from previous Jet Blue flights while a video camera rolled. Jet Blue re-created the cabin environment to help people remember past experiences and share meaningful information with the company.[1] In a separate research study, one marketing researcher went into malls and simply asked women to show her what was inside their purses. The experience told her volumes about the female consumers that so many companies are trying to understand and reach.[2]

Some brands commission researchers to gather specific consumer information. Other times, researchers do the work on their own and sell their findings to companies and advertising firms. Ad professionals use that consumer information when they are creating content seen on TV and the web, and in newspapers and magazines. Companies pay big bucks to understand what makes women tick and, most important, what makes them buy.

It's an elaborate game of Telephone. Women tell researchers who they are and what they want. Researchers relay that information to companies, marketing firms, and advertisers, who use the information to create savvy campaigns in the hope that women will pay attention, form a connection to their brand, buy their products, and remain loyal customers.

The business world plays this elaborate and expensive game of Telephone because they are working in an industry where scoring an advertising hit does not come easily. "It used to be the era that you would run a TV spot on one of the three networks and sales would go up," said researcher James Chung, president of Reach Advisors, a marketing firm that specializes in studying how consumers live, play, and buy. "Those were easy days." Since then, Chung said, three fundamental things have happened: The media has fragmented, consumers have grown numb to advertising, and companies are holding marketers more accountable for results. They want a quantifiable return on their investment.

Ad agency veteran Steve Hall agreed and explained that while media fragmentation has been snowballing since the advent of cable, it's fragmenting even more quickly now, due to the online community and the fact that people consume media on their own time, using TiVo and other DVRs [digital video recorders]. "Because the media landscape is a moving target, marketers sometimes grasp for straws in an attempt to stay ahead, trying to keep their head above water, as if they were drowning in a sea of never-ending media choices. One of the ways they deal with this endless change is research. They figure, 'Let's do a study; let's see what's happening.' It's an attempt to put some methodology behind the straw grasping," he said.

The first step in a marketing courtship is selecting a perfect mate, though it is not always easy for marketers to find their perfect woman. Women differ so greatly that there is no surefire way marketers can create a relevant message that resonates with all of their consumers, so companies first determine who their target consumer is. A target consumer is the type of woman most likely to buy a company's product, and therefore the one the company wants most to attract. While Clearasil is seeking teens and twentysomethings, Suave markets to young moms who are looking for some practical glamour in their lives. In determining their target customer and what would make her buy, marketing professionals start with the basics: learning who the target is, what she wants, and how she has been shaped throughout her lifetime.

Researchers have provided volumes of information about women. Age and generational data are key, since there are obvious distinctions between Baby Boomers (those born between 1946 and 1964), Generation X (those born between 1965 and 1979), and Generation Y (those born between 1980 and 2000). These years are rough estimates, as demographers have never come to a consensus on the exact time frames that define the generations.

According to generation expert Claire Raines, people are fundamentally shaped during their preteen years by the social and economic climates of that time, developing their beliefs and sensibilities based on the zeitgeist of the given era. For example, because Baby Boomers grew up in the post–World War II era, which was an optimistic, prosperous time, they tend to respond to optimistic marketing messages and are voracious consumers.

According to Matt Thornhill, a Baby Boomer market expert and a member of the Boomer generation, the post–World War II era "was a time in America when we saw the birth of suburbia. People moved out of cities and spread out, thanks to cars and the interstate. [Boomers] typically grew up in a neighborhood environment, where Mom and Dad started buying stuff to build the house." He noted that in the '50s, families were thrilled when new products—such as automatic dishwashers, washing machines, blenders, and television sets—came to the household. "As a result of that experience," he said, "Boomers became phenomenal consumers. If you wanted it, you could get it. We're all about personal gratification. *What's in it for me? How can I take care of myself?* Our parents taught us that behavior."

Author and Boomer market expert Mary Brown agreed that the prosperity of the '50s inspired Boomers. "Their core values are idealism, individualism, immediate gratification—and within that, Boomer women were raised to be self-aware and empowered, with a focus on self-actualization and self-expression," she said. A 2007 Botox commercial spoke directly to those women, telling them, "Don't hold back, express yourself by asking your doctor about Botox cosmetic. . . . It's all about freedom of expression." The women in the ads were also shown making facial expression, to illustrate that Botox doesn't restrict facial movement.

Consumers who are part of Generation X respond to different messages. This is in part because of the era they grew up in. During the late '70s and '80s, America was burdened with the Nixon scandal, stagflation, and high divorce rates. Many who are part of Generation X were considered "latchkey kids," as approximately 50 percent of them were left home alone after school while both parents worked. As a result, generational expert Claire Raines said, they became a generation known for self-reliance and cynicism. Marketers are aware that Generation X consumers respond to messages that speak to them as individuals, as well as to messages that drip with sarcasm. Sprite is believed to have risen to the fourth-best-selling soft drink (up from seventh) after appealing to Generation X by changing its slogan from the cheerful "I like the Sprite in you" to the more blunt and down-to-earth slogan "Image is nothing. Thirst is everything. Obey your thirst."[3]

Part of this cynicism is a hostility toward hype. In an article about Generation X, *Time* magazine wrote about a Nike ad that resonated with Gen X. The ad said, "Don't insult our intelligence. Tell us what it is. Tell us what it does. And don't play the National Anthem while you do it."[4] In a more recent example, a Gen X woman stares into the camera and says, "I don't buy into the whole 'magic pill' thing. When I quit smoking, I wanted something with a track record, so I got NicoDerm CQ."

Researchers who study Generation Y have generally concluded that these consumers are also skeptical of corporate America and hyped marketing messages, though while Gen X is jaded with corporate America, Gen Y has more optimism that companies will prove them wrong. Jim Farley, the vice president of Toyota's Scion division, once told a reporter, "They demand authenticity, respect for their time, and products built just for them. They are in their early twenties, new to us, and have changed every category they have touched so far. It's the most diverse generation ever seen."[5]

The World Wide Web has fundamentally shaped these young consumers. Generation Y consumers are sometimes described as sensory-overloaded multitaskers, adept at juggling cell phones, iPods, the web, and video games all at the same time. Because they consume so much media, Generation Y has become keen at ignoring any content they grow tired of, which includes advertisements. Marketers covet consumers in the Gen Y age group because they are at the time in their lives when they are trying new consumer products for the first time and are just beginning to develop brand loyalties. Younger consumers are also more willing to take risks and try new products and services—everything from a new snack like Flaming Fritos to a technology advancement like WiFi.

These young people are also known for being part of a collaborative generation, like the teamwork-oriented Baby Boomers. This is in part because Generation Y grew up watching how well the web worked when users contributed, whether by creating sites, blogging, or posting videos or comments. As a result, Gen Yers are more likely to appreciate companies with advertising campaigns that allow them to comment on, contribute to, and collaborate with their brands.

The burrito chain Chipotle Mexican Grill reached Gen Y by launching a video production contest for college students, awarding $20,000 to the applicant who created and produced the best Chipotle commercial. Chipotle then posted the winning ads on the file-sharing site YouTube, where they were viewed millions of times. Chipotle is a growing chain, but McDonald's is an investor—which could present a public relations problem for Chipotle, since many of its customers like the "little guy," boutique nature of the chain. To assure consumers that Chipotle is still one of the good guys on the corporate playground, the company often writes plainspoken, positive messages on its drink cups, reminding the public that it uses organic ingredients and naturally raised beef, and that it partners with smaller mom-and-pop farms. During a spring 2007 lunch at Chipotle, I saw that my cup had a message from the company on it. It said, "According to various media reports, Chipotle is now a 'chain.' (We thought we were just a burrito joint.) It simply means we have a lot of restaurants. But we're aware of the negative connotation of that word (we won't say it), and we're intent on disproving it by acting un-chain-like. Because big can be good . . . because of our size, we can influence for the better how livestock is raised."

Raines told me that Gen Yers are also known for having more friendly relationships with their parents. "They are good friends with their parents and their parents have taken on more of an advocacy role," Raines said, telling me that fewer Gen Yers see their parents as authorities and instead see them as peers. "I think it's because a lot of parents are Baby Boomers who waited to have children until later, and they wanted to do parenting differently." A commercial that reflects this change is a Special K commercial that shows a teenage daughter wearing her mom's low-cut bell-bottom jeans from the '70s. The daughter wears them day after day and is shown in quick snippets, each time with a new boy. Her mom doesn't look phased. She just steadily eats Special K. Soon enough, the mom has lost a few pounds and can fit back into those sexy jeans—and she asks her daughter to give them back. At the end of the commercial, the mom is shown coming down the stairs in them, looking ten years younger.

Generation is just one element that marketing professionals study when attempting to endear their brands to consumers. Gender is another. Researchers have concluded that women and men think, interact, and shop differently. So advertisers are recognizing those differences, using relevant language and images. According to the women's marketing consultancy Frank About Women, men shop linearly (with a goal in mind and making a decision quickly), but a woman's decision-making process is circular.

"Women don't go in with an end goal in mind every time," Frank About Women Executive Director Siobhan Olson said. "They ask a friend, check it out at a store, go back to that friend who can verify information. Then they gather more, [and] then they come back." For example, when the average guy buys shampoo, he makes his decision quickly and doesn't question it. When a woman tackles that same task, she can easily find herself standing in the haircare aisle for more than ten minutes, unscrewing a few bottles to smell the scents and comparing the product attributes and prices. She might wrestle with the question of whether a salon brand is more effective and worth the additional cost. An ad, coupon, or recommendation from a friend would weigh in her decision and help convince her that she is making the best choice.

Frank About Women's research has found that women invest more of themselves in their buying decisions. "After doing all the homework, if they are dissatisfied, it's almost like it's a personal reflection on their decision-making ability," Olson said. "It means that [companies] have to touch [these women] more times, and keep reinforcing it, or she will go [off] on another tangent."

Frank About Women encourages its clients to build what they call "touch points" into their marketing program, so that women experience the brand or product several times and can verify the messaging each time. For example, a brand selling laundry detergent could run ads in the newspaper and on television but also follow up with a supermarket display, a coupon by mail, an email, and an interactive website for the product. "They want to see it in action; they want to smell it, to open the bottle up—whereas men are more willing to buy if the logic is adding up. They don't question the end result," Olson said.

Women's market consultant and author Lisa Johnson pointed out that women and men also socialize differently, and that impacts the way they interpret marketing messages. Women, she explained, search for commonality with other women. Men, on the other hand, joke and one-up one another. As a result, advertising directed at men often involves a situation where men are outsmarting one another. But all too often, Johnson said, male bonding is inadvertently shoved into female-targeted ads. Think of all those commercials where the woman outsmarts her dumb husband or one-ups a group of male coworkers. Johnson believes these ads are created because male ad professionals neglect to consider how women bond, and instead brainstorm about what they think is funny and friendly. "[Male advertising executives] are applying their gender culture to us, and we don't play like that," Johnson said.

In addition to the traditional demographic research, a few more progressive groups of marketing professionals are going a step further, targeting women according to their level of social maturity. Carol Orsborn, from the communications firm Fleishman-Hillard, told me that her firm is utilizing a set of three archetypes that she created, based on the psychosocial stages of adult development. This, she explained, helps Fleishman-Hillard better understand the motivations, needs, and aspirations of women. Women who are considered Stage One in their adult development cling closely to the ideologies they were fed while growing up. These conventional women are usually loyal to their favorite brands, because they embrace the status quo and don't want to take risks. Orsborn said these women tend to take care of others, rarely consider their own needs, respect authority, and want authority figures to protect them. They tend to be drawn to companies that project a traditional image and take a more authoritative approach, keeping their products unchanged and including guarantees with their products. She believes the Oreck vacuum company has successfully appealed to Stage One women. Oreck ads show David Oreck as the authority, telling them about the dangers of mold spores, dust, and pollen. He also offers an eight-year warranty and a thirty-day home trial.[6] Clorox likely reached Stage One women through a 2007 commercial that illustrated how Clorox has been used for generations. The ad files through a series of fast-forward scenes, showing women washing clothes throughout time, from the old hand-crank machines to the machines of the '50s to the current stackable machines. The voice-over (a woman) spoke solemnly and said, "Laundry is not new. Your mother, your grandmother, her mother. They all did the laundry. Maybe even a man or two. And although a lot *has* changed—the machines, the detergents, the clothes themselves—one thing has not. The bleach most trusted to keep whites pure white is still Clorox bleach."

According to Orsborn, women who evolve to Stage Two in their adult development have grown beyond their original programming and are in a stage of transition and rebellion. These transitional women are rethinking the routine way they purchased products when they were in Stage One. They are trying new products and enjoying adventure. Women in this stage are also more mindful of their personal needs, Orsborn said. Marketing messages that resonate with these women remind them to take time out for themselves, and suggest that a new flavor, formulation, or brand is daring.

Women who reach Stage Three of adult development are at a point of self-actualization, Orsborn told me. This kind of woman will choose a new product because it *suits* her, rather than because it represents a risk. She also returns to some products she abandoned during Stage Two, taking a "best of" approach to her lifestyle and buying decisions.[7] Orsborn told me that women living in this aspirational stage tend to be older. These women are so comfortable with their life and purchasing choices that they are less swayed by marketing. "They are just as happy to go to generic if the value is there. They can't be fooled, so they want to be spoken to straight, and they don't want to waste time," Orsborn said. These women are also responding to messages of empowerment. Saturn reached Stage Three women with an ad that said, "I am a mother of two, but not just a mother of two. I am more than the sum of my errands."[8]

It makes sense to segment female consumers according to the stage they've reached in adult development, since women of the same age or socioeconomic background can behave and think quite differently. For example, a forty-five-year-old woman could be a new mother or a grand-mother. She could be a CEO or a college student. Her sensibilities could be based on her mother's beliefs, or she could be in a stage of rebellion. Ors-born and her coauthor, Mary Brown, believe women of all ages are experiencing life stages differently than those who came before them. Many twenty- and thirtysomethings, for example, are delaying marriage, parent-hood, and careers until their forties. This means they will also experience their forties and fifties differently, many in nontraditional ways. Because consumers no longer identify with their actual age, Orsborn and Brown have smartly implored marketers to reach women according to their life stages and the psychosocial stages of adult development.

These gender, generational, and sociological research profiles are just a few examples of how marketers get into the minds of their target customers. These are broad methods of segmentation. Individual companies also conduct more narrow research according to their product category. For example, a food manufacturer might study how thirtysomething moms and fortysomething moms differ when it comes to their snack-food needs. A company that makes cleaning products might study how women from various regions differ according to their worries about toxins or pollution. A clothing company that makes garments for Baby Boomers might use Orsborn and Brown's adult-development model and create three different ads to appeal to three different types of Boomer women. In the case of Jet Blue, the re-created Airline Booth research was done to learn more about how consumers specifically feel about Jet Blue.

Another way to understand consumers is through "persona labels," which represent a particular consumer identity based on the current era and very specific consumer motivations, habits, and lifestyle choices. Marketing firms commonly create and then release these identity labels, though the monikers rarely make it into the mainstream lexicon ("soccer mom" and "metrosexual" were exceptions). By and large, these terms reach only the marketing industry's ears, and sometimes they are helpful in identifying "types" of women out there. Consumer persona labels are not universally embraced by marketing professionals. Some, such as consultant Lisa Johnson, believe they lead marketers to think about consumers in narrow, stereotypical ways. Yet other marketers find them a useful tool for grasping the identities of today's consumers.

In 2004, the marketing firm Euro RSCG announced new categories of moms. Marian Salzman, Euro RSCG Worldwide's chief strategy officer, said, "We're seeing the categories of 'working moms' and 'stay-at-home moms' splinter into numerous segments as women depart from tradition to forge life paths that work for them." Euro RSCG created the following categories: Domestic Divas, Boomerang Moms, Yummy Mummies, Mini-Me Moms, and the Rage Brigade.

Boomerang Moms were described as working moms who quit their corporate jobs to become stay-at-home moms when their children reach their teen years. Maria Shriver was listed as an example of this kind of mom. Yummy Mummies were described as stay-at-home moms with high-earning husbands; these women focus more on their appearance than on domestic duties. Euro RSGC said the role model of the Yummy Mummy is British superstar and mother Victoria Beckham. The Rage Brigade was described as women who work outside the home and also handle many of the duties at home, therefore feeling rage against their husbands, who don't help out enough. Domestic Divas were described as women who want to appear as perfect homemakers, with perfect children and spotless homes; however, these women hire outside help to perform most of the homemaking duties, and spend most of their free time at the gym and other women's groups. Mini-Me Moms, Euro RSCG said, are control freaks who treat their children like fashion accessories and put most of their energy into molding their children into overachievers.

"These five categories by no means account for all moms in the United States," Salzman said. "There are plenty of other, more established categories into which women fall. What they do represent is a shift away from the more traditional models of the stay-at-home and working mothers. And I think we'll see even more splintering among moms in the future."

Similarly, in 2007, the marketing firm Consumer Eyes released nine new consumer personae. Consumer Eyes said each type has its own tangible consumer and media preferences, and for that reason, these labels "should be on every marketer's radar." Among the nine types are the Karma Queens, whom the firm described as Boomer ex-hippies who "pay attention to mind-body-spirit marketing" and drive quirkier automobiles such as the Volkswagen Beetle or Honda Element. Another type identified by the group are Parentocrats, described as parents who obsess over their children, multitask like crazy, and will buy only the best brands for their families.[9]

All of these labels are the result of consumer studies. Marketing and research firms, as well as retailers and manufacturers, are conducting this research to get into the consumer's brain. They are surveying everyday Americans over the phone, going into the homes of consumers for days at a time, watching consumers as they shop in stores, and building relationships with groups of consumers, whom they survey regularly. Each company chooses the research that works best for them, and each company's strategy is based on their findings.

The Lee Jeans Company is an example of the metaphorical scholar who studies up on his perfect girl and seduces her with effective advertising. In 2006, after fourteen studies about denim wearers, Lee unveiled a new line of jeans with the ad slogan New Fits, New Styles, New Lee.

"We pride ourselves on understanding who our consumer is," said Liz Cahill, vice president of marketing and communications for Lee. "You can't talk *at,* you have to talk *with* them. You have to understand what's important to them."

Cahill told me that Lee's message is rooted in being approachable, rather than ultra-aspirational. Throughout my interviews, I found that the word "aspiration" is thrown around a great deal in the marketing world. Many firms use the hook of aspiration to sell their products, showing slim, unattainably beautiful models. Cahill explained that this doesn't speak to Lee's consumers. "It's important that they don't see us as a crazy aspiration that is only something people in New York City wear."

Because Lee Jeans are sold in midtier department stores like JCPenney and Kohl's, Lee creates commercials that are believable to the women who shop in those stores. That is why the people who appear in the Lee commercials are attractive, but not exotic-looking models or drop-dead-gorgeous celebrities. "To show a fashion model or a celebrity wearing our brand is not as believable," Cahill said. "Women think, *Well, I know she doesn't shop where I shop.* So it's very important to be believable. Consumers are so smart these days, and they can see if you are trying too hard and not being true to the brand."

Lee is based in Kansas, where the company originated in 1889. Cahill believes this keeps executives like her grounded. "We are more in touch with our consumer than we are with the trends. Not that we don't know the trends . . . but first and foremost, we have to know what trend is important for *her*," she said, in reference to their target customer, which Lee defines as a woman 30 to 49 years old who is looking for traditional styling and comfortable jeans, but who also appreciates what Cahill called "a little bit of an update."

Lee's perfect girl also wears many hats. She has a busy lifestyle, kids at home, and maybe a job outside the home. Therefore, Lee believes, she does not have time to hassle with ill-fitting denim. At the same time, Cahill said, Lee's target customer doesn't want to give up and wear sweatpants. "She wants to feel put together. So if her best friend is wearing [designer] Joe's Jeans, she wants to feel comfortable [standing next to her]. She doesn't want to compare herself, but she wants to fit into the styling [of the designer labels]."

From its research, Lee is aware that the fit of its jeans is most important to its target consumer. "They compare [trying on jeans] with trying on a swimsuit," she said. In unveiling its Get What Fits campaign in 2006, Lee wanted to give women a reason to consider the brand again, showing them that Lee is playful and fun and is dedicated to making jeans that fit. Marketing firm Arnold Worldwide created a set of commercials geared to the core Lee Jeans customer using the Stevie Wonder song "Sir Duke" (with the lyrics "You can feel it all over . . . ") and showing a group of cute, approachable, thirty- and fortysomething models parading around in the jeans, dancing like it was 1985.

I wanted to see whether Lee's commercials scored. I spoke with a woman who fits the description of their target consumer, a forty-five-year-old nursing student and mother named Kay. Kay lives in Missouri and frequently shops at her local Kohl's store. She is a soft-spoken woman with a stern tone that tells me she's probably made prudent decisions throughout her life. She has conservative values, attends church regularly, and thinks women her age shouldn't try to dress like teenagers. She has a lot of angst about clothing stores and advertising. Neither suits her. Most ads she encounters are either too risqué or just boring; most clothing in the stores is either too youthful or too matronly. Kay considers herself in the middle and told me that corporate America doesn't recognize that part of the marketplace.

The Lee commercial was the exception. She loved the commercial's song, telling me that it reminded her of a song she heard in the past. She didn't realize that the song was originally released in 1976, when she was fifteen years old. And, true to Lee's research, Kay, unprovoked by me, wanted to talk about fit.

"I liked the thought that they might make jeans that fit me now," she said. Her only criticism was of the physiques of the women featured in the commercial. "The ladies were straight and skinny and not representing what real women look like," Kay said. Still, she countered, the commercial was fun ("but not overboard," she said), and it appeared to speak to women in her age group. "That seemed like a commercial made for me. I was ready to go out and see if they would fit me."

Even at her favorite stores, Kay can't find clothing that fits her size 16 body and is age appropriate. She used to wear Liz Claiborne, but those clothes no longer fit right. "They don't seem to get who I am anymore," she said of all the clothing companies and stores. "The women's department is like my kids' clothes. Career clothes don't look like career clothes anymore. Classic styles are gone." Kay most wants clothing to cover her up without making her look like a grandmother, she said, "and things that fit around my hips without making me look bigger."

She occasionally visits Coldwater Creek, a smaller women's chain that caters to the over-forty crowd and is decorated to look much more inviting than a traditional department store. "A couple of them have a water fountain inside, and the staff takes care of you. They help you find things," she said, pausing to add, "Like how Macy's used to be. It is a nice, friendly, fun experience. I don't find many things in there, but I do keep going back." Before I hung up with Kay, I asked her to try on a pair of Lee Jeans the next time she visited Kohl's. She made no promises.

Lee's commercials got the attention of *Advertising Age* columnist and ad reviewer Bob Garfield, who commented on the ads in his weekly column. He called the ads "utterly devoid of originality, wit, showmanship, attitude, or style," though he went on to praise the commercials for being utterly unhip, since anything more would alienate Lee's target consumer.

Garfield noted that the denim market has become incredibly niche. The Lee Jeans customer who shops at JCPenney and Kohl's likely has no desire to buy $300 jeans made by Joe's, Miss Sixty, or Paper Denim & Cloth. So the Lee customer and the designer customer should be courted differently. Garfield wrote, "Exactly how hip does a Kohl's shopper want her blue-jeans advertising to be? Permit me to answer: not very. There are vast swaths of America from border to border, coast to coast, who will never be in the market for Miss Sixty. They will never respond to edgy advertising, edgy design, or edgy anything."

Garfield contrasted the new Lee commercials with a previous Lee campaign created by a different ad firm, Fallon. That campaign, aimed more at men, featured a quirky character named Buddy Lee in an effort to bring a hip, edgy flair to the brand. Clever as they were, the ads didn't make Lee a growing brand, Garfield said. "The annals of advertising failure are strewn with hip, edgy, witty, original, memorable ads that brutalized the brand," Garfield wrote, "so should we not honor those who have given some thought to their audience?"

I must admit, the Lee commercials didn't inspire me to buy a pair of Lee Jeans, but I'm also not one of Lee's target customers. I don't shop at midtier department stores like Kohl's or Sears. Granted, I won't pay $250 for ultradesigner denim, though I'd happily drop $100 for jeans at Banana Republic. In fact, I like nearly everything about Banana Republic—the clothes, shoes, advertising, and the clean, preppy feel of the store. I even feel a strange connection with the other people shopping at my local store, because we all seem to identify with the style and want it for ourselves. Banana Republic just feels like me. Marketing consultant and author Lisa Johnson told me that it is natural for consumers to identify with a brand based on its advertising, marketing, and overall identity. Today consumers are taking this idea one step further, using brands as a way to form connections with like-minded people, whom Johnson called "twinsumers." "If I love Apple, I feel like the fact that I buy Apple tells you something about me. If I give you seven brands I buy, I've told you a story of who I am."

Thirtysomething Amy told me that four of the brands that define her are MAC, Coach, Tiffany, and Target. "To me it says, *I have taste, but I'm not over the top with my taste*" she said.

Fifty-four-year-old Barbara told me she loves Cascade and Dawn dishwashing detergent brands, as well as the Liz Claiborne clothing label. She explained that these brands are a reflection of her loyalty to certain tried-and-true products. "It's that green box," she said of Cascade. "It's that blue bottle," she said of Dawn, explaining that she equates quality with these flagship names and wouldn't trade them for any competitors.

For twentysomething Jackie, who is from Philadelphia and has played soccer since childhood, Adidas is part of her identity. "Everything I wear has to be Adidas. Every single thing: my shin guards, my cleats, my sneakers that I wear to work every day," she tells me. I asked her why. "Because that is, to me . . . the brand that says, *You're a soccer player. . . .*

I wouldn't consider another brand, because it doesn't seem real. Like, I wouldn't be as good of a player," she said.

My own favorite brands are Neutrogena, Saab, Target, Aveda, Starbucks, IKEA, and Jet Blue. What does this say about me? I'd say it means I value innovation, simplicity, and modern design—and that I have a caffeine fix.

In advertising, a brand reminds consumers what its identity is and how it differs from competitors. For example, Apple found great success with its 2006 and 2007 commercials, which show two actors, one portraying a Mac and the other portraying a PC. The actor playing the Mac is young, hip, and laid-back. The man playing the PC is overweight, dowdy, and irritable. By showing this comparison, Apple was able to reinforce its identity with consumers and draw in more like-minded hipsters. Target often produces ads that use popular music and computerized graphics, which contrast greatly with most of the folksy Wal-Mart ads. This distinguishes Target as the more modern big-box chain for people who don't want to shop at Wal-Mart.

Over the past decade, homogeneous department stores like Mervyns, Robinsons-May, and Macy's have lost their luster, as consumers have gravitated toward specialized stores with more distinct brand identities. Baby Boomer market expert Matt Thornhill said this rise in niche stores is due in part to more sophisticated technology over the past decade, as retailers have implemented bar codes and savvy computer systems. "Twenty years ago, there were no ways to manage and understand inventory," he said.

Since being able to easily monitor what sells, retailers have realized the benefits of segregating their products, developing more specific lines, and marketing them to segmented consumer groups.

There are now many national chains selling a very narrow range of merchandise. For example, some national chains only sell high-end cosmetics, such as Sephora and Ulta. Numerous clothing chains are devoted to narrow age groups, such as the 50-plus haven Coldwater Creek, the twentysomething outfitter American Eagle, and the tween-focused Limited Too. There are also national furniture chains that reflect a niche style of design, such as the Nantucket-inspired Pottery Barn and modern-skewing West Elm. Even big-box stores such as Wal-Mart and Best Buy are testing out niche versions of their signature stores to match the demographics of neighborhood locations.

Inside these stores, identity is king. Set one foot in a Coldwater Creek, Chico's, or Talbots store, and it's obvious that the stores are specifically for women over forty. Chico's is known for its bold colors and busy prints. Coldwater Creek carries more casual wear with an outdoor flair. Talbots carries more workplace clothing. As a workplace outfitter for Boomer women, Talbots ran the perfect ad in 2007, showing women walking around town in the clothes as the theme song from the *Mary Tyler Moore Show* ("You're Gonna Make It After All") ran in the background.

Urban Outfitters, Aeropostale, and American Eagle are chains specifically geared toward twentysomethings. Abercrombie & Fitch owns several different brands that reflect distinct identities to appeal to different young age groups. Abercrombie's beach-inspired Hollister stores are geared to the teen market. Its signature Abercrombie & Fitch stores reflect a more preppy, collegiate lifestyle. Its sophisticated Ruehl stores are for the post-collegiate set. In all of these stores, the interior design, salespeople, and merchandise reinforce the brand identity. Moreover, advertising is squarely targeted at young consumers. For example, in 2007 American Eagle inked a deal with the popular twentysomething actor Milo Ventimiglia to produce and direct a series of twelve three-minute comedy films featuring actors wearing American Eagle clothing. The American Eagle–sponsored films aired weekly on the company website, and a preview of the series ran in place of a commercial break during the 2007 season premiere of MTV's reality show *The Real World.*

"Niche marketing has been around for almost as long as advertising, but it has increased as advertisers have become savvy to the many worlds in which consumers operate and the many identities of American citizens," said Jennifer Scanlon, women's studies professor at Bowdoin College. "[We Americans] can now demonstrate our membership in a group not only through the clothes we wear, but through the ringtones we choose, the automobiles we drive, even the water we drink. As long as this approach is profitable, it will continue."

Mary Brown is a Baby Boomer consultant, a coauthor of *Boom,* and a Boomer herself. She said niche stores and brands have some upsides and downsides. "The more targeted you can be, the more potential you have to really think with particular consumer groups. And companies have had great success with it. But there is a danger," she said. "Boomer women don't think of themselves as old. I'm forty-eight, and I love Anthropologie. Coldwater Creek—yes, their clothes fit my body, but they feel too old for me. So, if a Boomer woman [senses that it's] older, or sniffs out that categorization, it can be a turnoff. The key is to really understand the persona, subsegments, and characteristics of the group you are going after. It's very tricky. You can't stereotype. . . . You can have a forty-five-year-old woman who has a newborn at home, one who's a widow, one who's a first-time grandmother."

It's amazing to me that a woman who is nearly twenty years my senior could be my twinsumer. But Mary Brown and I browse the racks of the same stores. Kay and I don't, though we both love Starbucks.

A few years ago, I sparked to a Gap commercial that showed young people in khakis dancing to swing music. It felt fresh and new to me, but to my grandmother, it harkened back to an earlier time. And not surprisingly, she and I both fell into the Gap. Nike got her too; she bought Nike shorts and athletic shirts for my grandfather. Thanks to an inclusive, timeless message from both companies, my grandparents never thought they were too old for the Gap and Nike.

Apple's message is similar. Many women over fifty told me that they love their Apple iPods. My own parents buy the neon-bright Bed Head hairstyling products and proudly display them on their bathroom counter. It's a whole new world in terms of age, identity, and consumerism, and that world is full of blurred lines.

Marketers, ever pressured to deliver results for their client companies, are searching for new ways to reach women and are finding that the game just keeps getting more complicated. Women are more diverse than they have ever been. They don't define their lives by their age. They are jumping on and off the career track to have children or explore other personal pursuits. They are replacing television with other sources of entertainment, like YouTube and other websites, video games, and cell-phone content. To meet the challenges, marketers have gotten more savvy about research, not only by just doing more studies, but also by evaluating more sophisticated segmentation models and incorporating brain research to determine how consumers process information in advertising.

Research is the first step. It's not enough to just be a gifted scholar. After doing all of the preparation, learning all they can about women, settling on their target customer, and creating an identity for their company, ad professionals still have to produce what is known in the industry as "creative," which are thirty-second television spots, billboards, print ads, and online ads. That content needs to seduce her and lure her in. This is no easy task. However, as you'll read in the upcoming chapters, smart firms are making progress by keeping their fingers on the pulse of popular culture, and by boldly taking risks.

CHAPTER 2

The Best Friend

The best friend has good intentions. He's been smitten with the girl next door his entire life, but he will settle for being her confidant—the person he shares inside jokes with and commiserates with in algebra class.

Marketers today are eager to become the best friend to their target consumers. Sociologists have told them that women tend to befriend one another in specific ways, and they are emulating those ways in their advertising approaches. "We look to build each other up," Lisa Johnson said of the main way women bond. "If you're in a car together, and the female driver is lost, you'll say, 'Oh, I get lost all the time too.' We try to identify. We like to relate to each other. We also compliment each other." Advertisers are simulating that kind of bonding by casting actors who look less like models and more like real people, in addition to creating ads that have relatable situations in them—all in hopes that women will befriend their brands.

It worked on me. Back in 2003, I began eating Special K cereal after I saw a commercial that featured a woman I could relate to completely: A cute, not-stick-skinny woman is waiting for the bus. It's morning, and cars, cabs, and people rush by her. She says nothing, but we can hear her stream of consciousness, which goes like this: *If manufacturers could get that they could cut it to be a size 12, but they just put a size 6 label on it, they'd sell so many more. All right, where is this bus? I cannot believe I missed the bus. I'm not stopping at the donut shop anymore; I mean, that's ridiculous. I'll go straight to the bakery, they're open early. . . .* Here she's interrupted, as she sees an attractive man on a bicycle ride by. *Oh hi, Mr. Man-with-the-Buns-and-the-Perfect-Calves. I could have calves like that. I have a treadmill . . . somewhere.*

The commercial ends by showing us a bowl of Special K cereal, while another person's voice reminds us that Special K is low in calories. A graphic also appears on the screen that says, "Don't be so hard on yourself." Previously, Kellogg's advertised its Special K cereal using stick thin models who wore the trademark red bathing suits. But in 2003, the company took a chance, went against type, and served its female customers this taste of reality. Special K and I began our friendship after that commercial, through the common denominator of that completely relatable woman.

Similarly, a series of 2006 Volkswagen Jetta commercials showed friends riding in the cars and having casual conversations, which are interrupted suddenly by high-impact crashes. The commercial flashes forward to a few minutes after the crash, as the occupants (safe from any injury) are surveying the damage and realizing the gravity of their situation. In each commercial, the driver of the Volkswagen begins to say, "Holy shit," though the commercial cuts off after the word "holy." We then see a graphic that reads, "Safe Happens." The ads were so successful that Volkswagen used the same high-impact crashes in the commercials for their Passat vehicles. "Our sales during the period (since the ads began) are up 17 percent over the last year. We saw it had a message that really resonated," said Kurt Schneider, VW's general manager of ad content.[1] After seeing those commercials, my friend Vivian, thirty-one and from Los Angeles, told me she thought the ads were relatable. "It was cool, because these friends are driving together, they aren't paying attention, and they get hit. That, I know, could happen." The VW commercials were a far cry from the typical car commercial, which Vivian described as "the ones where the car weaves around the mountain." She added, "I will never drive that fast on a deserted mountain." Another example of a car ad Vivian can't relate to is "one of these commercials where the car is weaving through downtown Los Angeles and it goes past the Disney Concert Hall, and they get out to go to the opera, and the woman has a long black gown on. I will never do that," she said. "I'm going to get hit at a stoplight before I'm going to any opera in a black gown."

When advertisers are trying to create realistic characters, situations, and conversations for their commercials, they draw on personal experience and seek help from researchers and consultants like Lisa Johnson. Her firm specializes in ethnographic research, observing women in their homes with their friends and family, rather than using the focus-group model, which she believes is outdated. "Instead of inviting women into a room with one-way glass and asking them to interact while we watch from the other side and eat M&Ms, we are saying, 'You guys do your thing, and we'll come to you,'" she said. "We changed how we listened."

Johnson travels around the country to meet groups of women, observing and interacting as a friend, while they eat pizza and share girl talk on a Friday night or go out for wine and cheese. Rather than stay in hotels, she stays overnight with a group of host women whom she can learn from. Sometimes there is even time for a slumber party, brunch, and morning coffee. It is at those times that she gets her best marketing inspiration.

"That's how you get stories," she said of the pizza parties, breakfasts, and potlucks where she listens as women candidly share funny memories, inspirations, and their inner streams of consciousness. She believes that the stories of these women can be translated into relevant, emotional advertising that other women will relate to. Johnson insists that the people and situations shown in today's advertising should be inspirational, authentic, quirky, and multidimensional, just like regular women. "That's why it's better to actually spend time with real women and see specific things about [them] and then focus on a specific life, [rather than going] with a bland composite."

The typical bland composite is what Johnson calls "female customer X." "Female customer X is this person we've never met, who we talk about in boardrooms. She has no personality, she is paper thin, she is built on a stack of stereotypes, and she's built from the perspective of what men think is funny about the differences between men and women," she told me. There are a few different versions of female customer X, Johnson explained. "There was the soccer mom. There was the cleaning fanatic in her khaki pants. There was the businesswoman. There was the cute young twentysomething with her horn-rimmed glasses. There was this little cast of paper-thin characters. . . . And after a while, you think, *She's fine,* but you don't say, 'That's me.'"

Johnson understands why companies cling to one-dimensional stereotypes and labels like the soccer mom. "[Women] are half the population, and stereotyping is a way to break it down. So it can be practical," she said. But Johnson believes these descriptions, in the end, lead marketers down the wrong path. "[Bland composites] lack the spirit that is behind women. Instead of expanding our view, they narrow it. [Marketers] hoped these labels would help [them] get a handle on things, and instead [they] strip [a woman] of her most wonderful qualities. [They] make her defined by a small set of things."

This is where marketers are, in Johnson's words, blowing it. "There are so many great little snippets from life. And instead, [they] are trying to be so literal and so formal," she said. For example, the phrase "soccer mom" doesn't conjure up positive feelings about women today. "No one would think of anything but her minivan and her orange slices. None of those names make us love her," she said.

Today, smart and effective marketers are replacing the bland composites with female characters who look and behave more like real women. The women portrayed in these ads have quirks and juxtaposition. For example, the now-defunct *Jane* magazine marketed itself in 2006 with an online banner ad that read, "Meet Jane. She writes her grandfather every week. She burps the alphabet. She's read Kafka. She's memorized *Zoolander*." *Jane* was primarily for twentysomething women interested in politics and culture and who have an irreverent, edgy streak.

Ads that speak to women as friends rather than consumers usually illustrate a human truth, which is a situation that shows a person's everyday experiences, hopes, memories, and/or vulnerabilities. It could be a woman's desire for doughnuts, or a group of friends' shock after being hit by another car. Vivian and I weren't the only ones lured in by a brand that befriended us. Thirty-four-year-old Jen, a single mom from Phoenix, found camaraderie through a string of commercials from Kleenex.

When I caught up with Jen, she was whizzing through traffic on her way from work to the grocery store. It was her only free moment before picking up her two children from daycare. When talk turned to advertising, Jen told me about a Kleenex commercial she saw that, in a documentary style, showed passersby being invited to sit on an outdoor sofa, impromptu, to share a moving life story as cameras rolled. Those who obliged spoke candidly. Some people laughed. Some wept. Many were shown wiping their wet eyes and blowing their noses. Kleenex's tagline was "Let it out."

"I just thought it was a good commercial, and it's important for people to let it out, because you're so much happier when you do," Jen said. I never met Jen in person, but just from our phone conversations, I could tell that she was one of those great down-to-earth women, the kind of gal who would help you rearrange the furniture in your house. Jen's got a hearty laugh and tells things like they are. And from the tired sound in her voice, I sensed that Jen was overworked, exhausted, and in need of letting it out.

"I'm definitely stressed and burned out. A lot of it is not having help, handling and managing everything. It's being the woman and having the curse of worrying about everything. You want to do a good job at work, but sometimes you really just don't feel like it. Your list is long, and sometimes you can multitask, but then I get frantic and I jump through my list, and then a little of everything is done, but nothing is actually off the list," she said. "You have so much going on, and at the same time, you want to add the extra things for the kids. And now it's dinnertime; what the hell am I going to make?"

Jen and her husband divorced in 2006, after ten years of marriage. She now lives down the street from him and said that life has only gotten busier. After working full-time for a local nonprofit, she usually picks up her children from daycare and takes them to after-school activities. Despite her more hectic schedule, the divorce has given Jen a new lease on life. "I think, for me, it's the fact that I didn't have a voice before, and now I'm out sharing things—and letting it out doing what I want to do," she said.

Not only did Kleenex stimulate Jen to release her daily stress, it also moved her with the stories its commercials shared. "You could feel the connection. You could feel what the people were feeling. One lady in the commercial was talking about never getting to meet her husband's mom because she had passed away. And my mom has passed away, so my kids, they will never have that connection with her. So I really felt what they were going through." These days, Jen is letting it out. And she bought the Kleenex.

Matt Crum, the director of North Atlantic Kleenex brand development, explained that the Let It Out ad campaign was unveiled to reinvigorate the brand. The previous campaign, created in 2000, was called Thank Goodness for Kleenex. It focused on an old advertising method that commonly showed the product solving a problem. Ads from that campaign showed Kleenex as a product used to clean up a stuffed-up nose, a messy sneeze, or watery eyes. When Kimberly-Clark (the company that owns Kleenex) surveyed people about Kleenex, the company commonly heard that the product was associated with being a high-quality, trusted tissue. The problem was that people's thoughts about the brand didn't go much deeper than that.

Kimberly-Clark shifted the focus from Kleenex as a problem solver to Kleenex as a product that encourages people to express themselves and be more human. "One of the things we say sometimes is, 'How do we go from being part of the furniture to being part of the family?'" Crum said. The company hired marketing firm JWT in New York to come up with a creative campaign to turn Kleenex into that family member.

Kimberly-Clark had already gathered research suggesting that consumers would embrace a campaign that showed expression and emotion. One survey showed that more than 80 percent of men and women think people keep their emotions too bottled up. Other data showed that people want to express themselves more, whether on email, in the company of friends, or on websites like YouTube and MySpace. All this gave the company clear signs that being expressive and authentic was "in," or, as Crum said in perfect business-speak, "We had some indications from the marketplace consumer trend standpoint that we were on-trend."

JWT came up with the phrase "Let it out." Kimberly-Clark tested the phrase and found that people responded enthusiastically to it. The company then hired a production company to travel to New York City, London, New Orleans, and San Francisco. They hired a friendly, balding, middle-aged man to ask strangers to share their stores on camera. They also brought in a bright blue sofa (a shade of blue that is one of Kleenex's branded colors). They plopped the sofa down in the middle of parks, city sidewalks, and suburban streets. On the adjacent coffee table was a box of Kleenex tissues. The balding man asked passersby to take a seat and chat with him. Surprisingly, many people obliged. He asked them about their happiest days, most heartbreaking moments, funniest memories, and most frustrating experiences. Within minutes, many people were reaching for Kleenex to wipe away tears of joy or pain.

"We want people to walk away and feel that Kleenex is a brand that encourages and believes in not bottling things up and [in] letting it out, and that we produce tools to do that in a comfortable setting," Crum said, referring not only to the tissues, but also to the Kleenex website, where visitors can blog and post videos to express themselves however they see fit. Crum admitted that the Let It Out concept was a huge step out of the brand's comfort zone, since it showed raw, real emotion. Some of the commercials show people looking vulnerable and even enraged. In the high-priced ad game, those kinds of emotions don't always sit well with focus groups and corporate executives, but Kimberly-Clark felt that Let It Out was worth the risk, especially given the current advertising climate. Crum pointed to the widespread use of digital video recorders such as TiVo—as well as audience fragmentation and fewer people watching TV (and therefore fewer commercials)—as evidence of a shrinking audience. Because it has become more difficult to reach consumers, the brand wanted to pack a bigger punch, and that meant allowing viewers to hear a real person's moving story instead of watching an actor fake-sneeze into a tissue.

I like the Kleenex brand because of Let It Out. I find that I stop my TiVo controller when I see a flash of the bright blue sofa on the screen. Like Jen, I want to hear those stories. And while I wouldn't consider Kleenex to be part of the family, it is most certainly not just a piece of the furniture. It is a friend. I can even recall tearing up when I watched a couple of the Let It Out commercials. One of them showed a woman from New Orleans who talked about losing friends in Hurricane Katrina and having to be strong. Sitting on the blue sofa, she told the man listening, "I'm still going to cry, though, because my tears don't compromise my strength. They never have."

While Special K and Volkswagen used actors to portray realistic, relatable situations, Kleenex utilized real people to make the ad look and feel even more authentic. No one capitalized on this recent trend more than Dove. Its Campaign for Real Beauty generated widespread attention by showing "real women" in its ads. In 2004, Dove unveiled its part change-the-world/part advertising campaign with billboards showing "real women" instead of models, many of whom were larger than a size 6, proudly bearing their curves in white cotton bras and panties. Similar to how the real people in the Kleenex ads revealed personal stories and raw emotion, the Dove women revealed their bodies, flaws and all. Glaxo-SmithKline also featured a real woman in commercials for the Commit Lozenge. The ads were produced to look like small slices from a reality show, following thirty-six-year-old Lisa through her daily life for several weeks as she quits smoking using the nicotine lozenge. Unlike most ads for smoking-cessation products, which allude that quitting smoking is simple, the commercials for the Commit Lozenge showed Lisa in frustrating, realistic situations where she is tempted to grab a cigarette. I recall one scene where she drives in her unglamorous minivan as her infant daughter wails in the backseat. Each ad shows Lisa struggling, but she never smokes again.

As an example of this sea change, Procter & Gamble rolled out a new ad campaign for its Always feminine products, and the company clearly decided it was safe to run commercials that frankly told women to "have a happy period." One print ad from the campaign told weary, period-ridden women, "This is the time of month that chocolate was created for. This is the time when no toenail should go unpolished. When the gym will get along just fine without you. This is the time when, if something is even slightly annoying, the world should know about it. And if you feel like crying, there is no inappropriate time or place. It's your period. You have the right to make it the best period it can possibly be. And we're here to help."

I thought the commercial was a more realistic way to talk about menstruation, but others I spoke to thought it proved that advertisers can go too far with candid talk. Thirty-year-old Andrea said, "Honestly, they gross me out and embarrass me in front of my family and friends. My kids do not need to know about 'that time of the month.' And when watching with my dad, he doesn't need to know I can have the fresh, feminine feeling. I understand we are 'different' women now than we were decades ago, but some things are still private."

Forty-four-year-old elementary school teacher Colleen also didn't like this campaign. She told me that the commercials were too explicit, and that most feminine-product ads take an annoyingly candid approach. "It's just, overall, getting so graphic about these products. There is nothing in the male world that exposes so much about a man's bodily functions," she said. The only thing comparable are the Viagra ads that talk about side effects, which include erections lasting longer than four hours. But again, that's something Colleen doesn't want her fifth-grade students hearing.

In 2006, Procter & Gamble showed real women revealing secrets in commercials for their Secret deodorant brand. The Share Your Secret campaign didn't mention perspiration once. Instead, the commercials showed women telling secrets to their moms, friends, and sisters. In one of them, two twentysomething friends—one blond and one brunette—were shown sitting next to one another. First we heard the blond ask the producer, "Are we ready?"—a sign to the audience that this shoot was real, not scripted. She then looked into her friend's eyes and said, "I feel like your best friend, Paul, is the one for me." Her brunette friend responded by saying, "Well, my secret is that Paul has asked me to help him look for an engagement ring for you." The women hugged and began crying. The commercial ended with the blond woman asking the producer, "Are we still on camera?"

In two other Secret commercials, young daughters tell secrets to their moms, secrets they seem ashamed of. A tween girl sheepishly admits to her mother that she got her first kiss recently while playing spin the bottle. In another commercial, a teenage girl sobs as she tells her mom that she wore her great-grandmother's wedding ring to a formal dance, where she lost it. She buries her head in her mom's shoulder as her surprised mom reacts and put her arms around her. Each of these commercials were full of awkward moments, making them difficult to watch at times. But with those awkward pauses came the awareness that real moments are awkward by nature.

Secret brand spokesman Jay Gooch told me that the women in the ads were revealing secrets on camera for the first time, and that nothing was scripted. Gooch explained that female consumers have long associated

Secret deodorant with feminine strength, due in large part to the brand's slogan, "Strong enough for a man but made for a woman," which was later adapted to "Strong enough for a woman," and then most recently to "Strong, like a woman."

"The idea is that it takes a lot of strength to share a secret," Gooch said of the concept. "Secret wanted to celebrate fifty years of feminine strength, and we were thinking of a way to bring that to life in a way that is meaningful." In doing so, Secret's longtime marketing firm, Leo Burnett, hired actresses but asked that each of the women not act on the day of the shoot. Instead, they were told to bring along a friend or family member to tell them an actual secret on camera. Gooch said all of the secrets revealed were shot in one take. The commercials all show a touching or hilarious moment shared between women.

The Secret ad campaign featured a website, Shareyoursecret.com, that included extended versions of these tapings, some of which followed the women after the shoot as they walked to their cars, telling the camera crew their departing thoughts. This website also invited visitors to share their own secrets online.

Gooch said the real reactions to the secrets on camera brought a level of genuineness and authenticity to the campaign. "We're also in a consumer environment where there is a lot of sharing going on," Gooch said, pointing to web communities like MySpace. "People are using technology to share and communicate in ways that are unprecedented, so if you think about it in the sociocultural context, the idea of sharing also works."

Other companies have invited consumers to interact with their brands by submitting personal stories. Method, which makes home cleaning products, created Comeclean.com, which allows visitors to reveal their secrets and read the confessions of others. In 2007, Shedd's Spread Country Crock asked consumers to go onto the company website to tell about a time they shared something with another person. For every story that was shared, Shedd's donated a meal to the charity America's Second Harvest. That same year, Neutrogena promoted its new Mineral Sheers Blush makeup by asking women to log on to Neutrogena's website and tell about an embarrassing moment that made them blush. The person whose story was selected by Neutrogena won an all-expenses-paid vacation. These sharing moments are perfect opportunities for companies to connect with consumers. Naturally, after a woman spends thirty minutes writing to a brand and sharing her personal story, she is likely to feel more invested in that brand. And, of course, compelling stories could easily become the inspiration for the company's next commercial.

Real people and relatable experiences are being used in today's advertising landscape in part because this approach has become quite popular in today's entertainment media landscape. We live in a reality-focused world, thanks to reality television shows, more honest discussion on women's talk shows, and file sharing on websites such as MySpace and YouTube.

As marketing veteran and *Inc.* magazine columnist Adam Hanft said in an interview with me, we are living in a "confessional culture," which has sparked an unprecedented honesty in female-targeted marketing. The phrase "confessional culture" likely stems from the MTV program *The Real World.* Since 1992, the program has chronicled the lives of seven young strangers who are chosen to live together in a house and have their lives taped. Often the housemates seek out private time in an enclosed room of the house, affectionately called the Confessional. While inside, they speak directly to a camera, venting their innermost feelings about life and their fellow housemates.

The Real World and its beloved confessional spawned a trend of real people and real talk in entertainment. After watching *Real World* housemates bicker about dirty dishes and wonder aloud about their successes and failures in life, American audiences grew more intrigued with the lives of other real people. From 2000 to the present, other reality shows such as *Survivor* and *The Apprentice* have achieved mass appeal. In addition, game shows made a resurgence with such shows as *Who Wants to Be a Millionaire, Deal or No Deal,* and *Are You Smarter Than a Fifth Grader?* Few reality and game shows are rooted in reality, and most people don't watch these programs looking for inspiration to be more open and authentic; however, candor has been a by-product of these shows, as well as an interest in real people, as opposed to characters portrayed by actors.

America had already been primed by talk shows such as *Donahue* and *The Oprah Winfrey Show,* which brought more private issues to the forefront and featured real people on panels. In the '90s and into the new millennium, talk show hosts began sharing more nitty-gritty details about their private lives. In 2006, Oprah took cameras with her on a road trip across the country with her best friend, Gayle, allowing the American audience to watch as they sang, bickered, and slept in their car. Morning hosts like Kelly Ripa, Meredith Vieira, Barbara Walters, and Elisabeth Hasselbeck frequently share humorous details about their children and their home lives. With the help of Oprah Winfrey's doctor, Mehmet Oz, who is a frequent guest on her program, Oprah delved into more private medical topics, allowing her audience to ask Oz very personal questions, like "Why is my poop brown?" and "How much sex should I be having each month?"

Rosie O'Donnell commented about the changed television landscape when she first joined *The View* in the fall of 2006. Thinking back to her original daytime talk show, *The Rosie O'Donnell Show,* which ended in 2002, O'Donnell said, "I did a show for six years; I never said 'vagina' once. I've been on this show six days; we have said 'vagina' ninety-four times." A year later, shortly after Whoopi Goldberg became the moderator of *The View,* the women of the panel were even more comfortable talking about the female anatomy. During a conversation about faking orgasms, Barbara Walters said the word "clitoris" several times.

Everyday women have adopted that same honesty, and thanks to the web, they are confessing their daily frustrations and triumphs through blogs, MySpace pages, and YouTube, as well as in their conversations with one another.

Andrea is a thirty-year-old stay-at-home mom in Phoenix and a friend of Jen, the woman I interviewed over the phone about the Kleenex Let It Out campaign. Andrea told me, "I think my generation speaks more openly with our friends about sex, our relationships, our children, sharing personal catastrophes. Society has made it easier to share these things. They are just out there. When my mom got a divorce, it wasn't talked about. It was a shameful thing. Whereas now, people are having happy hours to celebrate it."

Amy Richards and Jennifer Baumgardner, coauthors of the book *Manifesta,* believe the trend in "real talk" and "letting it out" is due in part to increased opportunities for women. "Women felt, in the 1950s and '60s, that other people are making decisions for you," Richards said. "Things have really changed. It's still stressful. There's still pressure. But there are a lot more women having a fuller range of options." Baumgardner explained that women thirty years ago could not share their difficult moments or even joke about their frustrations, because they weren't in power positions. As women have achieved those power positions, the lines of frank communication have opened. When Richards and Baumgardner were writing their book, about how women in their teens, twenties, and thirties were embracing feminism today, they learned about a regular feature in *Seventeen* magazine called "Traumarama," which allows teen readers to describe their most embarrassing moments. "We wondered, why are you talking about this? What are women getting from this? It's so masochistic," Baumgardner said. Richards and Baumgardner were stunned to learn that young women found "Traumarama" to be empowering. "They [told us] 'It makes you feel like you aren't alone.'"

Relatable stories are all over magazines today. Many times, female periodicals like *O* magazine, *Every Day with Rachal Ray, Real Simple, Marie Claire, Domino,* and *Martha Stewart Living* include stories of everyday women who are chosen for their artistic mastery, entrepreneurial success, perseverance, or humanitarian work. Regular women are also shown in photo shoots, further illustrating that female consumers today want to read inspirational stories about women like them.

Ads are following the trend, with real people, real stories, real secrets, and real struggles. And when actors are used in commercials, they more often look like real people than like perfectly coiffed actors. At a party, I got into a conversation with Hollywood agent Shana Randell, who told me that she sends her actor clients out for commercial auditions on a daily basis. She estimated that 70 percent of the casting calls she receives specifically ask for actors who are "very real, nonactor types." "They want people you can relate to," Randell told me. As a result, Randell advises the actors she represents to take commercial headshots that show them looking casual, with little makeup and primping.

Tesia, a twenty-seven-year-old African American, recently took a class to learn how to audition for television shows and commercials. She was told by an instructor that she should keep her hair natural, as opposed to having it relaxed or adding hair extensions. Tesia believes this could be because many more African American women today are wearing their hair natural. Therefore, casting directors would be more likely to hire her to star in a commercial if she looked less like a model and more like an everyday woman. "It used to always be the stereotypical Barbie doll–type women in ads, but now [advertisers] are looking for everyday people, so that you say, 'This person reminds me of myself,'" she said.

Laura, thirty-six, from Brooklyn, has also noticed more real women in ads. She told me about a series of print advertisements she saw that showed real people from interesting walks of life modeling the clothes. "They were trying to take interesting women from a diverse range of ages and in interesting careers. They included an artist, a musician, and a boxer—women in jobs that are 'outside the box.' So, instead of portraying the everywoman as an advertiser would conceive of her, they showed real people," she said. Laura didn't know which company did this, but she said the ad caused her stop and look at it longer. "If I don't know who the people [in the ad] are, I read the fine print. Because if they were picked, it's for a reason, whereas if it was some generic actress, I would flip the page. It's like, 'Oh, this is an architect wearing these clothes, and I've never seen this hoodie and khakis. Maybe I should try this on,'" she said.

Certainly, women are still moved to buy products after seeing celebrities in advertisements, but now real people are also packing a punch. In our celebrity-focused culture, some consumers have been desensitized by star power and are becoming more inclined to stop and look at an ad that highlights real, everyday people with interesting life stories. Studies also show that consumers are less likely to trust celebrities. A 2006 Harris Poll found that 69 percent of the Americans surveyed said they did not trust actors to tell the truth. In fact, actors received the lowest trust score of all the professions included in the survey. Bottom line: Consumers are looking for trustworthy messages from real people, instead of endorsements by actors who are paid off.

If a brand is trying to win my loyalty and my dollars with a classic courtship technique, I'm far more likely to trust the relatable women from Kleenex, Special K, and Secret over a Don Juan. But in today's advertising landscape, there are far more Don Juans than friends. Consumers are jaded. I found that many of the women I interviewed could deconstruct ads down to the bare bones, telling me what they believed was fake, exaggerated, and just plain false. Even Laura—who told me that the clothing ads she saw were effective because they showed real people—also expressed some skepticism, saying, "They are taking real people and trying to convince you that their brand is about real people, when it is really just as staged." For some consumers, even the use of real people seems false and manufactured. But for women who respond strongly to a sense of camaraderie in advertising—real or staged—the "best friend" approach stands a good chance.

CHAPTER 3

The Fan

The fan has an endless enthusiasm for his woman's way of life. She is his muse. His life revolves around her as she picks up new interests, changes her routine, and updates her style. He follows her path, speaks her lingo, and shares her passions.

Marketers know that women are in a constant state of flux, and that their opinions and lifestyles change along with the times. So part of their job is to play the fan, taking cues from those shifts and reflecting the current world in their advertising.

In my interview with Liz Cahill, vice president of marketing and communications for Lee, I recalled her mentioning that after 9/11, Lee's research revealed that women were more family-focused, staying home more, nesting, and going back to things that made them feel safe—which included familiar brands. "You see things like that happen in society, and it really does shape the marketplace. And you really have to be in tune with that," she said. Research expires quickly as world events, pop culture trends, and daily news reshape the zeitgeist and, as a result, consumers.

As childhood obesity and diabetes became an epidemic in the 2000s, Americans—especially women—became more aware of nutrition and the dangers of processed food, fast food, and high-fructose corn syrup. Surveys showed that Americans were increasingly concerned about nutrition and health. For example, a 2005 Gallup Poll found that nearly half of Americans were worried about their weight.[1] As a result, many companies—especially those with food and healthcare products—updated their advertising messages to dovetail with this new awareness, touting taste less and talking more about the healthy, natural qualities of their products. In 2007, a Hellmann's/Best Foods commercial reminded consumers that its mayonnaise is made of basic ingredients: oil, eggs, and vinegar. Print ads proudly said, "It's time we all said no to overprocessed food. It's time for real." Similarly, 7UP told consumers that its soda has no artificial flavors or preservatives. The commercials showed cans of 7UP in a field, growing on a vine. Sales went up 18 percent in the first quarter following the release of the new ads. Kelli Freeman, vice president of marketing for 7UP, told *USA Today,* "We haven't seen consistent growth like that in several years."[2]

In another example, the 2000s saw a revival in do-it-yourself projects. Interest rates allowed more people to buy homes, and at the same time home-improvement television shows, such as *Trading Spaces* and *Extreme Home Makeover,* became popular. The user-friendly nature of the web also led more people to abandon professionals such as insurance agents, accountants, and real estate agents, instead doing this work themselves. The business world followed that trend, releasing commercials that empowered consumers. The Home Depot's slogan "You can do it; we can help" was particularly relevant. An Oil of Olay commercial told women that they didn't need to see a plastic surgeon to have collagen injected into their lips. All they needed was Olay's Anti-Aging Lip Treatment, which was simple to apply and achieved the same result. Commercials for Crest Pro-Health toothpaste and the Oral-B Pulsar Pro-Health toothbrush tell consumers that the products give teeth the feeling of a professional cleaning. TurboTax commercials told consumers it was a cinch to do their own taxes.

In addition, industries that lost business as a result of this shift fought back in advertising, attempting to prove their worth. A Century 21 commercial showed a real estate agent speaking directly to the camera. She said, "Some people think they can do it all on the computer: find a home, sell a home. Except the computer can't do what I do at Century 21: understand your needs, the subtleties of the market, the neighborhood, the schools, the process. . . . No computer can do that."

Some ads have immediately responded to current events. After Don Imus made disparaging comments about the African American players on the Rutgers University women's basketball team, Nike took out a full-page ad in *The New York Times* that said, "Thank you, ignorance. . . . " This was followed by statements such as "for moving women's sport forward" and "for making us realize we all have a long way to go." Even the celebrity tabloid culture and popularity of Paris Hilton were reflected in an ad. The ice-cream chain Cold Stone Creamery produced a humorous ad in 2007 that showed two rich young heiresses staring one another down as they carried their teacup–size dogs. Similarly, a 2007 Saturn Vue commercial showed a spoiled young socialite who bears a striking resemblance to Paris Hilton as she jaywalks across the street, oblivious to the cars driving by because she is busy with her cell phone, shopping bags, and small dog. She walks in front of a moving Saturn Vue, but the driver is able to stop on a dime. This commercial was a part of a series of Saturn ads that spoke to consumers who are fed up with the overindulgence of Hollywood and bigger-is-better Americanism. A Saturn commercial showed images of diamonds and stretch SUV–style limousines, while a graphic read, "Just because you have money doesn't mean you have to waste it." Each commercial ended with the tagline "Rethink American."

In addition to topical trends, other social forces steer marketing. For example, one social force currently guiding marketing strategies is the way Baby Boomers, and women in particular, are redefining aging. Marketing consultant, author, and Baby Boomer expert Mary Brown explained to me in an interview that developments in medicine, nutrition, and fitness have led to people living longer, and living more youthful midlives. "What actually has happened is that a decade has been added to midlife. There is another whole decade where the quality of life is really good. People fifty to seventy years old tend to be very active," she said.

I found this to be true in my talks with just a few Boomer women.

Sixtysomething mom Gayle, who lives in the California desert near Nevada, said that while women in their fifties and sixties aren't thrilled about aging, they are less fearful than previous generations because of advances in medicine and cosmetics. "We feel that there are a lot of breakthroughs. We all have parents in their eighties and nineties, so for a lot of us, we feel we have a lot of life still ahead of us." Forty-five-year-old Kay, from Kansas City, went from being a housewife to being a nursing student in her forties, and in 2007 she took a two-week trip to Jamaica to care for the sick in a clinic in one of the roughest parts of the island. As she prepared to leave for the trip, she told me, "This is probably one of the most adventurous things I've ever done."

Surveys also reflect Boomers' changing attitudes and media habits. A recent survey asked people under fifty "How old is old?" The average answer given was sixty-eight. For Boomers over the age of fifty, the average answer was seventy-eight.[3] An online survey by the Boomer-focused communications agency JWT Boom revealed that, of the 45-plus people who use the web, more than 72 percent access it through a broadband connection in their home, rather than through a dial-up modem. JWT Boom concluded that 89 percent of Boomers typically visit a website after seeing a print ad, and 83 percent visit a site after seeing a television ad.

In the past, the most coveted demographic to marketers has been people aged 18 to 49. As consumers have aged into their fifties, marketers have spent less money reaching them because the commonly held assumption has been that people who are 50-plus spend less, are less likely to try new brands and products, and are less inclined to use technology. However, new studies are revealing that today's Boomers are actually voracious consumers, eager to switch brands, use technology, and spend money in large numbers. JWT Boom estimates that people age, 45-plus comprise over 40 percent of the population and have 70 percent of U.S. net worth, controlling $9 trillion. JWT also believes that the 50- to 62-year-old age group will grow by 50 percent over the next fifteen years, compared with the 18- to 40-year-old age group (Generations X and Y), which JWT projects will only grow by 3 percent.[4]

In 2007, the huge consumer-products corporation Unilever announced its completion of an exhaustive study revealing that Boomers would indeed spend more than previous retirees. Unilever initiated the study, entitled The Boomer Project, in part to show ad executives that Boomers were indeed worth pursuing. "When we first started launching this project internally, we received emails from some of our younger colleagues asking, 'Who cares about these people?'" Mike Twitty, Unilever's senior group research manager in the Shopper Insights division, told *Advertising Age* magazine: "[They talked] as if Boomers were already over the hill and not very important. Their contention was that they don't buy a lot of our products. It was just that knee-jerk reaction that does not reflect the data."[5]

Matt Thornhill, a consultant on the Boomer market, explained some of the reasons this knee-jerk reaction exists in the marketing world. "For the last thirty to forty years, it was all about the youth—because it was all about Boomers, because they were young." Thornhill told me that the prime 18-to-49 demographic was developed when Baby Boomers matured into that age range. Consumers outside that demographic weren't nearly as desirable, and that is now hurting Boomers.

"In many respects, Boomers have created their own nightmare," Mary Brown said, explaining that in their younger years, Boomers questioned authority and didn't trust anyone who was old. "Their obsession with youth has, ironically, stayed put as they have aged," she said. Research shows that Boomers are feeling left out of the fold. A survey conducted for the TV Land cable network found that 45 percent of Boomers say they are overlooked by marketers who advertise on TV. Three out of four Baby Boomers surveyed by TV Land said they would pay more attention to commercials that portray situations they can relate to.

The marketing industry's lack of understanding about and interest in 50-plus consumers is also likely due to the demographics of many ad shops. Ad veteran Steve Hall told me, "Advertising agencies are made up of one kind of person. It's the hipster New York City twenty- or thirtysomething—which represents a small portion of the population." Hall explained that the industry has long been known as a young person's game. "At forty-three, I'm way too old to go work at an ad agency. There is hardly anyone older than forty. It's a very young thing—a twenty- to thirtysomething kind of business. If anyone is older than that, they fall into one of three categories. Either they own their business; they are an old young person, who dresses, acts, and thinks young; or they are a wannabe. They might look young, but they are out of touch and are just playing the part."

Hall also told me that he believes young urban ad professionals want their work to reflect them, and so they often strive for their work to look young and speak to young people. "Everyone out shooting a commercial would rather be shooting a movie. They are out there with ulterior motives. There's this desire to be cool and not seem uncool. They have their own personal agenda, and their work reflects them, so they, of course, want to create something they would deem cool," he said.

Marketing consultant Kimberly McCall agreed that the "cool factor" often prevents advertisers from remembering their target consumers, be they people who are 50-plus or people living in suburban or rural areas. "You've got to know where to hunt for your food. That may not be aesthetically pleasing for your sensibility, but that does not matter." She later said, "Marketers are, for the most part, savvy. We live in urban areas. A person who lives and makes their living in Manhattan, Los Angeles, or Chicago is a completely different human than someone who lives in Kansas or Maine. As a creative person, for me, it's all about the beauty of the ad. But it's really about speaking to the target audience in a language they understand. It doesn't matter if it's not sophisticated to [my] sensibilities."

Research is showing that Boomers, and Boomer women in particular, are worth reconsidering. Boomer women, like all women, are most likely to be in control of the spending in their households. At the same time, Boomer households are most likely to have the most discretionary funds. Marti Barletta—author, Baby Boomer market expert, and founder of the firm TrendSite Group—says this is because Boomers have worked for the previous few decades and accumulated wealth, and are still working. "They are in their peak income years. These are the senior vice presidents at companies. They have the top-paying jobs in their lifetime," she said.

Mary Brown said that women encounter many life-stage changes during their Boomer years, which make them attractive targets for advertisers. Her company conducted a study that showed that women between 50 and 54 years of age are actually experiencing more life-stage transitions than any other age group. Their children are often going away to college, while they might be getting a divorce, going back to college, experiencing menopause, dealing with the death of a partner, and/or caring for aging parents. "When faced with new challenges, they are looking for solutions. That is where marketing comes in. If your brand message speaks to how you can solve a life-stage problem, it's a great opportunity to speak to consumers. That's not to say that everybody isn't always going through life changes, but it really revs up in your fifties and sixties."

Larry Jones, president of the TV Land cable network, which has created programming for the 40-plus demographic, told *Advertising Age,* "We've definitely seen changes in the last two years. Three years ago, the preponderance of advertisers out there were targeting 18 to 49. Today more and more have started buying into the 25 to 54 demo[graphic], because [that demographic] has the biggest pile of money, and it is growing faster than the 18 to 49 money." Still others argue that Boomers are not being considered by particular industries. "There is still a great deal of discrimination against women in this age group in the fashion and technology areas," said Brenda Sage Darling, the vice president and publisher of *More* magazine, which targets 50-plus women. "They look at 18 to 34, and that's their cutoff point."[6]

Barletta believes that when advertisers do market to Boomers, they focus too much on anti-aging. Her own research reflects that Boomers aren't as concerned about aging as the media makes them out to be. "What happens is, everyone who writes about Boomers says [they] are in denial, and they will do anything not to get older. They are 100 percent wrong about that. Baby Boomers, women included—all of the language that we have to describe them comes freighted with such negative baggage. But it's not at all a denial of being older," Barletta said. According to her, Boomer women are simply denying the *false* label that they are passive, gray, boring, inactive, toddling, ill, or uninteresting because of their age.

Barletta's most recent book, *PrimeTime Women,* explores the myths the business world holds about aging, and how Boomer women are breaking that mold. She came up with the term "primetime women" because she believes women between the ages of 50 and 70 are in their prime, both in their personal lives and as consumers. She explained that this is an age when many women change their focus from the family to themselves and truly discover their authentic selves in the process. Barletta says this is a time that Boomer women often refer to as "my time."

Eager to increase sales, companies are learning from consultants like Barletta, Brown, and Thornhill. The companies are doing their own research and creating up-to-date commercials to reach Boomers. Unilever is in hot pursuit of Boomer women with Dove's ProAge line of cosmetics, specially formulated for 50-plus women, with advertising that speaks positively about aging and tastefully shows Boomer-age women in the nude. Ameriprise Financial ran a 2007 commercial showing Dennis Hopper standing on the beach with a dictionary. Speaking directly to the camera, he said, "To withdraw. To go away. To disappear. That's how the dictionary defines 'retirement.' Time to redefine. Your generation is definitely not headed for bingo night. In fact, you could write a book about how you're going to turn retirement upside down . . . because I just don't see you playing shuffleboard."

The challenge of being the fan is to stay ahead of the game and to tap into trends as they are happening. The marketing firm DDB created a cutting-edge research program called SignBank to keep its finger on the pulse of local, regional, and global trends and large-scale behavioral shifts. I went to DDB's Los Angeles office to learn more about how Sign-Bank works.

DDB's lobby looks just as I imagined it would—studded with stainless steel furniture, which is accented with modern fabrics. An Emmy award that the company won in 2005 for Best Commercial stands proudly on a display pedestal encased in Plexiglas. Space age–looking televisions are set in the walls behind the reception desk, each running a continuous loop of commercials created by the firm.

The reception area seems to be the epicenter of the company. There, I watched a stream of attractive young people scamper back and forth, all of them focused on their own projects. As Steve Hall and Kimberly McCall told me, advertising is a young person's game. This is not only because of the long hours and workload, but also because younger employees are believed to better understand how to reach the coveted 18- to 34-year-old demographic. The employees at DDB confirm this theory. They all look to be in their twenties and thirties, dressed very cool in skinny jeans, layered hoodies and jackets, geek-chic glasses, and brightly colored designer tennis shoes.

DDB is a scholar, but it's also a fan. The firm believes its creative professionals can generate stronger marketing and ad campaigns by keeping on top of trends and cultural changes. DDB's SignBank program allows the firm to identify these shifts as they are happening, and no later.

Here's how the program works: DDB's thirteen-thousand employees worldwide are the program's eyes and ears. Throughout their everyday lives, they take mental notes of slight behavior changes and emerging societal quirks in their communities. At work, they document those "signs" on Post-it notes or in emails, and send that information to the SignBank department of their local DDB branch. SignBank's regional managers organize the signs and help make connections to forecast trends.

The signs are then filtered to SignBank headquarters in Copenhagen, where sociologists analyze the signs coming from DDB offices around the world. It can take months or years for SignBank to come to conclusions about big societal trends. SignBank reports are given to DDB's creative advertising executives to help them when developing ad campaigns.

"Oftentimes, colleagues might think a sign they saw was silly, but they report it anyway, and often there are similar signs coming in from other regions of an area or even on a global scale," said Eva Steensig, the global leader of SignBank. Steensig explained that the idea for SignBank was hatched when the company realized that current marketing research techniques have limitations. "I think there are a lot of problems with how marketers do [traditional] research," Steensig said, referring to normal focus-group sessions where people sit in a room and are asked their opinions. "The quantitative data is nice, but you can only ask about the things you know. So it confirms what you already know. It is backward looking. It doesn't help you detect change."

Instead, SignBank research focuses on what people *do,* rather than what they say they *want* to do while they are in a focus-group session. SignBank also studies the actions of people throughout their daily lives, as opposed to studying them only when they are acting as consumers, which is, on average, only 3 percent of the day, Steensig said.

Jennifer Dellapina manages the Los Angeles office for SignBank. She explained that her colleagues are constantly thinking about societal quirks, and that they come into her office to talk about them. She helps connect those signs to others, and she passes that data on to Steensig. "For example, we're noticing that people are using Crock-Pots again,"

Dellapina told me, wondering if there could be some kind of retro 1970s fascination in the zeitgeist, which would dovetail with recent movie remakes such as *The Dukes of Hazzard* and *Starsky and Hutch*. Dellapina walked me through a recent SignBank report, which found that Americans are living in what SignBank calls a "my-crosphere," embracing their numerous choices, be it "my vote on *American Idol*," or "my choice to buy an item recommended by Amazon.com." The SignBank report also cited a trend in entitlement, finding that Americans have higher-than-ever expectations in all areas of their lives. Dellapina said SignBank came to this conclusion upon connecting several signs, such as the high rate of credit card debt, the popularity of counterfeit designer handbags, the rise in older children living with their parents, and the growth of no-money-down home loans. These trend reports, which guide the advertisements that DDB's creative professionals generate, all stemmed from signs originally identified by DDB employees.

In another example, DDB employees worldwide recognized that women were dressing more provocatively at work, showing more skin, and dressing more femininely in general. After many months of putting together the pieces, SignBank concluded that while the sexual revolution technically took place in the '60s, it is still going on right now. SignBank believes women have become more explicit and comfortable about their femininity and sexuality because women are more empowered globally.

After monitoring numerous signs coming in from various branches of DDB offices worldwide, Steensig and her team of sociologists were able to conclude that femininity is no longer a sign of weakness, and that a growing number of women have reached positions that previously have only been reached by men.

SignBank's report cited numerous examples. More women are reaching high leadership positions in the business world. Many are also being elected to political office. In the U.K., there are more women than men who are millionaires in the 18- to 44-year-old age bracket. The majority of Malaysian career women are opening their own savings accounts, unbeknownst to their husbands. In American universities, the majority of students are female. Changes in the Middle East are slight; however SignBank employees in Bahrain and Oman reported that the style of the *abaya* (the long black Arabic garment many women wear) has changed ever so slightly. All of these global signs led Steensig and her team to conclude that women are gaining more status in the world and can thus express themselves as they want.

"They don't have to look like men to be heard or taken seriously, so they rest more heavily on their femininity and use it more comfortably," Steensig said, adding that in past decades, women had to actually remove their femininity and gender to get their power, which partially took away what it meant to be a woman. Now that the world is experiencing true women's liberation, women can exhibit their femininity, both in terms of dress and in their social skills, without fearing they will lose respect from colleagues or peers. As Steensig said, "They don't have to sacrifice half of their identity."

When I spoke to thirtysomething mom Jody, who lives in a Virginia suburb, I found that she reflected SignBank's findings. Jody holds a bachelor's degree in journalism, but after just a couple of years working in the field, she chose to become a stay-at-home mom. When I asked her why, she replied, "Women have qualities of nurturing that are in them, and why not honor them?" Though she has experienced moments of self-doubt and bits of criticism from family members and neighbors, Jody told me she is proud of her decision: "It is okay to be a mom."

Jody married soon after college. After completing an internship in a newsroom, she decided that the long hours at work would not be conducive to childrearing on her terms. It wasn't long before she was pregnant, and she decided to trade news reporting for stay-at-home motherhood. Jody explained that she actually always wanted this life, but resisted it because she worried it would disappoint her parents. She was especially influenced by her mother, who was stirred by the women's liberation movement of the '60s. "My mom had a negative image of the housewife," Jody told me, remembering what her mother would tell her as a child: "Girls can do anything that boys can do.' I was hounded [with that] my whole life growing up. I was this daughter of the '70s, and, you know, 'You can go out there and fight a war,' and I was like, 'I don't know, do I really need that? Or is it okay to be a mom?'"

Research from SignBank, numerous other marketing research firms, and the U.S. Census has shown that there is a growing number of women choosing to stay home with children. This research is also shedding light on what is motivating this choice. According to the U.S. Census Bureau in 2002, almost eleven million children under the age of fifteen who are in two-parent homes are being raised by stay-at-home moms—a 13 percent increase from the previous decade.[7] While in the past stay-at-home motherhood might have been thought of as conservative and dowdy, today it's trendy.

James Chung, with the marketing research firm ReachAdvisors, was part of a study that examined stay-at-home moms. Chung explained to me that after the start of World War II, the number of women who returned to the workforce rose steadily about 1 percent each year until the late '90s. "Since then it's been dropping. People have been trying to figure out why," he said. One theory is that people tend to shift away from how they were raised. Since today's young mothers—mostly part of Generation X—were known for being latchkey kids with working parents, these moms may be opting to stay home as a reaction to their own upbringing. But Chung said there are other factors. "When we pick apart the numbers of who is staying at home, it's heavily concentrated in the women on the highest economic end." Most of those women are married to college-educated men who can support the household independently. Those women are often college-educated themselves. Overall, the college attendance rate has soared over the past two decades: In 1975, 50 percent of high school graduates nationwide went to college. Today, 86 percent attend.[8]

In addition, college-educated women are more likely to have left the towns where they grew up, which may lead to their decision to stay at home to raise children. "[These women] are finding that it is hard to raise a family away from that infrastructure," Chung said, explaining that extended families often help working mothers take care of the children. A college education also gives women more confidence that they could leave their job and get another one later. "So it's less of the 'Have it all' generation," Chung said, repeating that famous (or infamous) phrase of the '70s and '80s. "They want what they want, and they are willing to take turns in sequence to get it. 'Have it all' was such a mantra at the time, and you don't hear that anymore."

Companies are aware that women's perceptions of motherhood are changing. And in classic fan fashion, they are reflecting those sensibilities in their advertising. Consider a 2006 Mitsubishi commercial that showed a hip young married couple looking for a car at a dealership. Their names were never mentioned in the commercial, but let's call them Josh and Jane. Josh has his heart set on the Mitsubishi Endeavor, a large sport utility vehicle. Jane isn't so sure she likes it. Josh is frustrated that he can't immediately convince Jane. He looks to Larry, his friendly Mitsubishi dealer, for help. Just as Jane looks away, Larry the dealer plays a game of pantomime with Josh, motioning like he's cradling a baby in his arms. Josh gets the hint. He turns to unsuspecting Jane and says, "It's the perfect fit for that family we've been talking about." That is just what Jane has been waiting to hear. She blissfully wraps her arms around Josh. They will buy the car and start their family.

After watching that commercial—and having not yet done the research for this book—I was baffled. I wondered why the folks at Mitsubishi would risk annoying women—their core buyers—by poking fun at our biological clocks. What exactly was Mitsubishi trying to say to women? Are we so desperate to have children that we are putty in our husbands' hands anytime they dangle the prospect of a baby in front of our faces? Did Mitsubishi really want us to think their dealers are so slimy that they would team up with our husbands to dupe us? My first call was to Marylou Quinlan, an author and marketing expert, whose firm Just Ask a Woman gathers women to share their opinions in a talk show format. This is another way to avoid the typical focus group, guinea-pig style of research. Quinlan reminded me that advertising is all about targeting, and companies are in hot pursuit of women in the 18- to 34-year-old category. She explained that women in this age group, primarily those in their twenties, likely wouldn't be offended by the Mitsubishi commercial. It is a different era. "If you did this commercial twenty years ago, women who watched a commercial where their maternal instincts were being played on would be irritated," she said. "Today, women are more comfortable with the choices they have, whether it's being a mom or being a career woman or both, and therefore, talking to her as a potential mom is pressing a real positive hot button."

I later spoke with an executive from the Deutsche Agency, whose company created the ad for Mitsubishi. He confirmed that women in the focus groups who viewed the commercial before it hit the airwaves had no negative reactions to it. Most of the women who watched the ad thought it was funny and, most important, real. I described the Mitsubishi commercial to Amy Richards and Jennifer Baumgardner, coauthors of the book *Manifesta: Young Women, Feminism, and the Future*. Neither of them found the ad offensive, though they could understand why feminists might have picketed at Mitsubishi had the ad run twenty years ago.

"There was a great deal of idealism in the '80s," Richards said. "This was also a relatively new concept—women being in control. Therefore, any challenge to that would have felt more regressive. Today, I think we know that we can embrace tradition and yet still be political, smart people. What we do and how our household is organized doesn't necessarily undermine who we are as people. I also think that women today can have more of a sense of humor about these things, mostly just because to not have humor gives 'the other side' too much power."

Richards and Baumgardner, both thirty-seven years old, studied women in their teens, twenties, and thirties when writing their book. Based on their research, they concluded that young women still believe in the principles of the women's movement but express feminism differently today. "You don't have to go somewhere to be a feminist. You can be one where you are," Richards said, later adding, "It's not about standing on the outside, yelling. It's just different. It is evolved. Just because it isn't covered by *The New York Times* doesn't mean it isn't happening."

Even the word "feminist" isn't used by younger women. According to a 2001 study conducted for *American Demographics* magazine by the New York City–based youth market research firm Element, only 34 percent of participating girls aged 13 to 20 labeled themselves feminists, yet 97 percent believed a woman should receive the same pay for the same work a man does. This disparity exists among women as a whole, not just young women. A 2001 Gallup Poll asked women of all ages about their opinions about feminism and labels. More than two-thirds of women said they disagreed with the statement that men and women have equal job opportunities in the United States. Thirty-seven percent said they are dissatisfied with society's treatment of women. However, only 25 percent of these women said that they identify themselves as feminists. This applied nearly equally to older and younger women: 26 percent of younger women and 24 percent of women over the age of fifty identified themselves as feminists.

Kristin Rowe-Finkbeiner, author of *The F Word: Feminism in Jeopardy—Women, Politics, and the Future,* told Salon.com about a poll she conducted for her book. Three hundred college-educated women between the ages of 18 and 34 were asked their opinions about various labels, including feminism. Rowe-Finkbeiner said, "Sixty-eight percent of young women didn't want to be confined by labels, and the word 'feminism' chafed the worst." In the introduction to her book, Rowe-Finkbeiner wrote about Traci, a twentysomething from the South, who said, "When I think of feminists, I think of those women who are totally against men. I wouldn't want to be labeled as a feminist. Actually, I don't like labels at all. I just want to be me and have my own opinions."[9] Similarly, a college student named Natalie, a University of Michigan junior, told *The American Prospect* magazine in 2003: "I would not call myself a feminist. I'm experiencing a lot of the advantages that feminists worked to achieve, and I'm thankful. . . . But I don't know that women are still that much uneven from men, especially in the workplace."[10]

Forty-seven-year-old mom Melanie lives near Chattanooga, Tennessee, and holds a college degree. She stayed at home with her three sons for many years. In my interview with her, she said that women and men are now on a more equal playing field. "I think that 'feminist' still has kind of a negative connotation—the strident, militant woman with a chip on her shoulder. The benefits of the feminist movement are more subtle: having confidence in one's own abilities and worth as a woman, with strengths and flaws."

Jody, the aforementioned thirtysomething who left a career in journalism to be a stay-at-home mom, enjoys her days with her boys, viewing it as a magical time that, while challenging, is full of moments meant to be savored. She is even a bit sad to drop off her oldest boy at elementary school. She wonders what she'll do with her extra time when both of her sons are in school all day.

Commercials are reflecting the very best of what motherhood has to offer, which today's stay-at-home moms are embracing. One Johnson & Johnson commercial, shot in nostalgic black-and-white, simply showed a mom contentedly giving her baby a bath in the kitchen sink. The commercial was casual and relaxed and felt like a home video, and an acoustic version of a lullaby played in the background. The voice-over said, "You always went for the tall, dark, handsome types. So who'd have ever thought the love of your life would be short and bald? Having a baby changes everything." Similarly, a series of Kellogg's Rice Krispies commercials, also shot in black-and-white, showed special moments between mothers and children taking the time to eat breakfast and marvel at the wonder of the crackling sound of the cereal. In one commercial, a mom and her four-year-old daughter eat cereal and give each other Eskimo kisses as the voice-over says, "The best Mother's Day gifts are usually the simple ones."

Young women are also redefining what a mom looks and acts like. "The phraseology of the 'soccer mom' has disappeared," said Chung. "You see this visceral negative reaction to it. Moms aren't one-dimensional. They don't feel as one-dimensional as they've been told they've been in the past." Indeed, stay-at-home moms like Jody are more likely to reject the stereotype of the drab soccer mom. They use the words "hip" and "cool" to describe themselves instead. "We still have the minivan or the SUV, and we still are moms. But just because we are moms doesn't mean that we don't want to feel sexy," Jody said, telling me about her monthly Moms' Night Out, when the ladies get dressed up and go out for dinner. "It's funny, because we have men come to the table, flirting, and they realize we are a mom's group and are like, 'Really?'" she said with a bit of glee in her voice.

Suave tapped into this need for moms to feel sexy with an advertising campaign, unveiled in 2006, called Say Yes to Beautiful. It reminds them that motherhood and womanhood can coexist in their everyday lives, and encourages moms to put beauty back on their "to do" list. Because Suave has always been considered a low-cost brand, Suave's new twist positions itself as a guilt-free beauty solution for moms.

Say Yes to Beautiful is completely geared toward moms, as opposed to women in general. One commercial proclaimed, "Have sexy two-seater hair in your minivan life. Say yes to beautiful without paying the price." Another commercial showed a mother's life captured in fast-forward motion, illustrating her transformation from a put-together single woman to a haggard mother of three. At the end, she is instantly transformed, with glossy hair, lipstick, and a smile, courtesy of Suave.

Sarah Jensen, director at Unilever Hair Care (Suave is a Unilever brand), discussed this approach in my interview with her. "We know through our research that many moms have let their appearance slide since having children. And while this is a tough realization for many moms, the fact is that 100 percent of moms can get themselves back." Suave research found that the average mom ranks cleaning the floors higher on her list of priorities than doing her hair, and she devotes 87.9 minutes a day to meals and only 4.2 minutes to her hair. "We know our target [customer] loves being a mom—she wouldn't trade that role for the world. But we want to shake her up a little and remind her to look in the mirror and think about her own beauty," Jensen said.

The website for Suave.com reinforces the Say Yes to Beautiful message. As it loads, the homepage reads, "You are about to enter a playground for moms. A place where you can put carpool, homework, and dinner on hold and say yes to beauty and yourself. It's a place where you can let the pretty woman inside you out to play without an ounce of guilt. So go ahead, say yes to beautiful." The site includes tips from a group of style mavens, which Suave calls its Momtourage (likely taken from the ultra-cool HBO show *Entourage*). Website visitors have submitted their real-life stories about motherhood. Suave's online community of moms voted for their favorite stories, which were then produced into sketches acted by *King of Queens* star Leah Remini. The Suave website even includes a pledge for moms to print, sign, and presumably hang on the fridge. It reads, "Today I will say yes to 'Mommy, you look pretty today.' I will say yes to my curls, my highlights, my bangs, my shoulders, knees, and toes. Yes to a vanilla-scented shower. Yes to wearing sexy two-seater hair to drive carpool. Yes to the fact that I'm a woman as well as a mom. And I will say no to feeling one ounce of guilt." Suave's messaging is striking a chord with moms. Sales were up 3 percent in the first quarter following the campaign's launch.[11] Suave told me that since the first quarter, sales have continued to grow, though the company wouldn't give me specific percentages.

Suave's message is also aimed at moms who are mindful of their own needs and identities beyond motherhood. This too is a trend, and is being reflected in advertising. "The mom has moved to [being] a mom with an attitude. She wants it known that she isn't all about house and kids. She draws lines," women's marketing consultant and author Marylou Quinlan told me. Andrea Learned, who is also a women's marketing expert and author, described the portrayals of today's mom, saying, "She doesn't just stay home and make sure her husband's shirts are white, or bake cookies." These are the little nuances of reaching women.

Some moms respond to the ultranurturing, mommy-focused message of Rice Krispies. Others want to be spoken to as women, not moms. Kevin Burke is president of Lucid Marketing, a company focused solely on reaching moms for its clients. "[Moms] want to feel that the company 'gets it.' 'They understand me, they understand my life.' And most companies don't get it," Burke said. "One of the keys is that it's not always about speaking to her as a mom. Sometimes it's just about speaking to her as a woman with marketing messages. Sometimes there is too much emphasis on her as a mom. What [women] don't like is overstereotyping."

While Jody, mentioned previously in this chapter, is most proud of her role as mother, she too wanted me to understand that there is more to her being than motherhood alone. Over time, she said, her husband began to see her only as a mom, which in part led to marital problems. Jody still believes that marriages are more likely to fail when both spouses work, though she also wonders whether her choice to get pregnant soon after marriage and stay home strained her union with her husband. "I think back to before I got married, and I think he looked at me differently. Now I'm lumped into this I'm-just-a-wife-and-mother-thing." Jody compared her situation with that of her friends in her mother's playgroup. "They worked longer, and it seems to be less of a problem," Jody said, "probably because the husband had more time around her while she was a working woman, and he had that sense of [her] identity."

Jody gave an example of how her husband's narrow perspective of her identity has become problematic. Her husband goes to bed early, at about the same time the children go to bed. He wants her to go to bed at the same time they do. "He couldn't understand that my day doesn't have to end when his does. I love that time at night to have some tea, clean up the house, sit down and veg, check my email. He just could not understand that," she said. "He's lost track that I am a person outside of being a wife and mom."

A 2006 Suave commercial recognized that moms are struggling with identity and, as a result, sometimes feel nonexistent. It showed an invisible woman performing daily tasks, such as grocery shopping and housework. The voice-over said, "There are moments every mom feels invisible. That 'invisible mom' feeling doesn't have to apply to your hair. Say yes to beautiful without paying the price." Women reacted very differently to the commercial. Online, I found a few angry people blogging about it. One person wrote, "Let's review: Women's work is invisible and clearly not valued. The problem? Clearly women aren't looking 'pretty' enough. All your (very political) woes will be solved if you just make your hair shinier/fuller/straighter . . . that whole undervaluing of your work is just natural. So don't worry about that." Another web posting simply said, "Way to talk down to your target audience. Idiots!" My single friend Elana called me in a rage after seeing the commercial, wondering aloud why a commercial would portray moms as invisible.

Unilever Hair Care Director Sarah Jensen responded to that criticism by saying that the Say Yes to Beautiful campaign issues direct and playful wake-up calls. And some women found reality in that approach. On a website (not Suave's) that serves as an online community for moms, one woman wrote that she enjoyed blogging on the web: "I think that we want to make sure that what we are doing for so many hours of our week is not invisible, because, as the Suave ad says, we often feel invisible. It's sort of an 'I blog, therefore I am' thing."

Jody wishes other people recognized stay-at-home-momdom as a respectable profession, no less important than being a lawyer, teacher, or executive. Jody recalls one specific article on the web that explained how stay-at-home moms can respond to people when they ask the dreaded question: What do you do for a living?

"A lot of moms say, 'Oh, I just stay home,'" Jody said. "Then one day somebody said to me, 'Oh, you're just a homemaker,' and I said, 'No, I'm a domestic engineer; I manage a household, and I do all the accounting. I do this, I do that. . . ' The person didn't really get it." Jody recently saw a commercial for Colgate toothpaste, featuring Brooke Shields. At the end of the commercial, Shields alludes to her children when she says, "I spend my days face-to-face with some very important people." It is one of Jody's favorite commercials, because she feels it legitimizes her work: taking care of the children. She considers that to be her primary job. She resents that housework is automatically considered part of the stay-at-home mom's duties, and that her husband expects her to clean the house because she stays home. She told me about a print ad she saw in a magazine for a housecleaning company. "It was for Molly Maids, I think. It was a woman. She had her briefcase, and her house was a mess, and she had this look on her face. And it said something like, 'Take a break, call Molly Maids,' and I wondered, why can't it be a stay-at-home mom in the ad? Just because she stays at home doesn't mean she doesn't want someone else to clean her house."

In the case of all of these mom-targeted ads, I found that trend-watching doesn't guarantee women will relate to an ad. For example, Jody has moments when she wants advertisers to speak to her as a nurturing mother, and other times when she wants to be spoken to solely as a woman. She generally wants to see hipper portrayals of mothers in advertising, though other women I spoke to didn't find hip mamas to be realistic or compelling.

"I don't think it's accurate," said stay-at-home mom Andrea, thirty and from Phoenix. "You know, in ads, if it is a mother, she is always fit; her kids are always clean and look good. And it's just not how life is. I come out with my ponytail. I don't wash my hair every day. I'm not a size 6, and I never will be," she said, telling me she identifies more with the crazed mom whose kids are making a mess. Thirtysomething Taguhi, who relocated from Los Angeles to South Bend, Indiana, said that moms in the Midwest look a little different from the ones in Hollywood, as well as from those in ads. "They are more like Roseanne than Sarah Jessica Parker, and obviously that isn't portrayed in advertising."

Melanie, the aforementioned fortysomething stay-at-home mom, lives near Chattanooga, Tennessee. She agreed. "Thinking of California women, the ads aren't that far from the truth, but if you look at women in the Midwest and South—yes, the ads would need to have more women who looked like Roseanne in order to be realistic. I don't think of myself as anything 'hot,' but when I look around me at the grocery store here, or in Burger King, I feel like a supermodel sometimes." Melanie told me that when she was a younger mom, the "soccer mom" image didn't have such a bad connotation, and she still doesn't mind it. Not surprisingly, Melanie wasn't moved by Suave's hip-mom commercials. She prefers their old marketing sales pitch. "Their old catch line was 'Suave does what theirs does for a lot less.' That's my philosophy," she told me. "Get my hair clean and don't charge me too much for it."

Moms weren't the only ones who found inaccuracies in the portrayals of women in ads. Childless wives and single women had qualms with the commercials they saw. Some wanted to know why so many commercials pair gorgeous, capable women with overweight, childish men. Thirty-year-old Stacey, a single Idaho transplant living in Southern California, said, "It really has started to get to me the more I notice it. The hip mom is doing everything, and she is frazzled and she is snapping at her husband, who is this cutesy character," Stacey said.

Just browsing through commercials one afternoon, I found a handful of examples. A commercial for the discount store Ross shows a husband practicing his golf swing in a fancy restaurant as his embarrassed wife rolls her eyes. A Baskin-Robbins commercial shows a mother and father reprimanding their son for bad behavior. The mother adds that they won't be going to Baskin-Robbins, as was previously planned that day. The father responds childishly, "Whoa, let's not go crazy here." (Baskin-Robbins also ran a commercial showing a stern dad and fun-loving mom. It was the only time I've seen the flipped scenario in a commercial.) In a Lowe's commercial, a wife tries to convince her weakling husband to retile the bathroom as he fakes a cough and grumbles at the same time, "Too hard to install." She finally drags him to the store, where an employee shows them how easy it is. At the end, he coughs into his hand and admits, "You were right." In a DiGiorno pizza commercial, an overweight husband and his group of immature friends sit on lawn chairs in the front yard, watching television and eating snacks. When the wife returns from running errands, the husband asks her to bring out a pizza. In the end, she turns on the sprinklers to seek her revenge.

I already knew Lisa Johnson's theory that the "dumb dad" joke in advertising occurs because male creative executives draw their inspiration from the teasing and one-upping bonding habits that come naturally to them. However, advertisers are also fans. That means they are looking at what is politically correct in current society, in addition to monitoring the comedic themes used in entertainment media, such as prime-time television and movies. Family sitcoms of the '90s and 2000s most often revolve around an inept husband and smartass wife. Gone are the days of the zany housewife and down-to-earth husband, as seen in shows like *I Love Lucy* and *I Dream of Jeannie*. Gone are the days of the strong father figures in '70s and '80s sitcoms like *The Brady Bunch, The Cosby Show, Family Ties,* and *Growing Pains.* TV husbands today are most often portrayed as overgrown children, both in children's programming and prime-time sitcoms (in both syndicated reruns and current shows) such as *Home Improvement, Everybody Loves Raymond, King of Queens, According to Jim, Family Guy,* and *The Simpsons.* Hollywood has done this as well with films such as *The Break-Up, Wild Hogs, Knocked Up,* and *Old School.*

The "dumb dad" is likely commonplace in today's media in part because of the current state of political correctness. As advertising executive Marian Salzman, coauthor of the book *The Future of Men,* told one reporter, "Political correctness means that nobody except for a straight white man can be a doofus."[12] The prevalence of the "dumb dad" has led to the creation of a consumer-advocacy website called Fathersandhusbands.org, which is calling for more positive images of men in advertising and the rest of the media. A 2007 survey conducted by that group shows that men portrayed in prime-time television, both in ads and programs, are viewed as poor parents, sources of marital discontent, and stupid in general. It also showed that wives in commercials and television shows are often shown as being justifiably dissatisfied with their husbands.

"Women like thinking they have the upper hand, and we were taught that we've never had that. That is why these ads are so effective," Tracie Snitker, a spokeswoman for the Men's Health Network, told

Women's Quarterly magazine in 2001. "There is definitely a poor image out there of men. These kinds of campaigns are subtle, but they do pervade our inner consciousness."[13]

The obvious deduction is that these ads hurt men and bolster women, though I believe they hurt the image of women just as much as they do men, because they imply that women commonly settle for mediocre partners, and that women would rather be married to immature fools than remain single or get divorced. Many of the women I interviewed said the ads also imply that wives and mothers are wet blankets who refuse to have fun. Colorado wife and mother Miranda, who has been married more than ten years, agreed, saying, "It's overdone and tiresome, and quite often makes the woman look like an overbearing bitch—the woman who can't lighten up or enjoy life and move more fluidly through the day. That's the message I often see implied when the dumb, fun-loving husband is dancing on the couch, rather than finishing the taxes."

As single thirtysomething Stacey (mentioned previously in this chapter) told me, "What you get from these ads is, *This isn't the kind of woman you want to be.*" Fortysomething Melanie (also mentioned previously in this chapter), who has been married for more than twenty years, found the ads to be "totally unrealistic." She continued, "I know that there are helpless husbands out there, but seeing them on TV is just kind of irritating." She said it was even more irritating to see stupid moms and dads on the children's programs that her youngest son watches, such as *Jimmy Neutron, The Fairly OddParents,* and *Hannah Montana.*

Thankfully, it appears that the "dumb dad" is dying out in current television programming, since family sitcoms are growing far less popular. More often we are seeing quirky, likable, smart women in leading roles on prime-time programs, such as *Ugly Betty, Thirty Rock, The Closer,* and *The New Adventures of Old Christine.* The hope is that the fans of the advertising world will stay on top of the television trends and have the courage to replace the "irritable wife" portrayals in advertising with likable, smart women.

That's the thing about the fan—he's a brain, similar to the scholar, but he's also a maverick—the first person in the chain to warn his corporate client that the consumer has changed and moved on to something new; the first to encourage the team to change course and follow along with it. It takes courage to stop using dumb dads in favor of just using smart, witty, self-assured women—especially when few marketers have gone there yet. It's risky to begin speaking to moms and Boomers differently when few companies are doing it. But firms like DDB and corporations like Unilever are going out on a limb, with thinking-outside-the-box research studies and programs. Consumers, and women in particular, appreciate companies that reflect their changing attitudes and lifestyles, and that have the resources and fearlessness to stay current.

CHAPTER 4

The Player

The player on campus is the guy who knows where all the cliques hang out, and he strategically places himself there. If he's smitten with a girl, he hangs out by her locker at the time she is scheduled to stop by. He knows who is dating whom, who is available, and who is new on campus.

Marketers act like the player because it is simply their job to know where women spend their time. For many decades, women have shared a common hangout: their living rooms, where they watch television. As a result, many companies run their ads on network television during the times and programs that help them reach their target audience. For example, commercials for gyms and diet programs like Weight Watchers frequently air in January, when many people are sticking to their New Year's resolutions. In the morning, during *The Today Show* or *Good Morning America,* commercials tend to appeal to both working and nonworking watchers, featuring broad-reaching products such as headache medicine, blockbuster movies, and automobiles. At 10:00 AM, as *The View* and *Martha Stewart* begin, commercials for diapers and peanut butter appear for the stay-at-home parents who are still at home. On programs known for attracting affluent, educated audiences, such as the now-canceled NBC show *The West Wing,* ads for high-end products like luxury cars and computers are common.

When it comes to commercials, advertising professionals mainly examine a television show, network, and time of day to select the best place for their thirty-second spots. But broadcast television is losing its hangout luster, and that is making the player's job more difficult. According to the ratings-data guru Nielsen, the network television audience has eroded an average of 2 percent each year over the past ten years, even as the population in the United States has increased by thirty million.[1] Consumers are being drawn away by new entertainment hubs, such as cable TV, the web, video games, and even cell phones. Marketers are eager to understand how consumers choose where to go for entertainment and how long they stick around. In ad-speak, these choices are called a consumer's "media consumption habits."

Statistics are showing that, of all the hubs available, the web is the most popular new medium being consumed. A 2005 Harris Poll found that 74 percent of all U.S. adults—an estimated 163 million people—use the web, up from 57 percent in 2000 and 9 percent in 1995.[2] A 2007 survey from Edison Media Research asked consumers which form of media was most essential to them. While television got the highest marks, garnering 36 percent of the responses, the web was right on its heels, receiving 33 percent of the vote. Edison compared that data with a similar survey done in 2002 to show how the web's popularity has grown in just five years. Back then, only 20 percent of people surveyed said the web was the most essential medium.

More important, the Pew Research Center has shed light on how women consume the web. The Pew Internet & American Life Project found that in the 1990s, during the early years of the Internet, more men than women used the web; however, by 2000, men and women were using the web in equal numbers, and this continues today. Pew found that while men enjoy the web for the experiences it offers, such as entertainment and recreation, women enjoy the web for the human connections it fosters through email and online communities.[3]

In addition to reducing the number of hours spent watching TV, communities such as Facebook and MySpace have also led consumers to read fewer magazines. And because more magazines are targeted toward women than toward men, these Internet trends have had a noticeable impact on advertising tactics for women's magazines. As Nat Ives wrote in *Advertising Age,* "It's not that young women are completely abandoning magazines, it's that they've added other types of media. And advertisers have had to follow them—meaning advertising budgets for print that once went toward three or four titles in the field may now be directed at only the top one or two in order to free up money for emerging media."[4] It's led to magazine closures, such as the demise of *ElleGirl, Jane,* and *Cocktail*

Weekly. Other magazine publishers, such as *People,* are reaching magazine readers who are spending time on the web by producing online versions of their magazines, called digimags.

Each year, companies are diverting more of their ad dollars to the web. TNS Media Intelligence estimated that ad spending on the web in 2007 would grow by 16 percent over the previous year. However, they estimated that spending on cable television would grow by only 6 percent, network television would grow by only 1 percent, and newspapers and radio would see declines.[5] Marketers are testing a variety of email initiatives, online advertisements, and interactive activities to reach women in connective ways on popular websites and blogs. In addition to banner and spot ads on websites, companies are creating viral videos, as well as fifteen- and thirty-second commercials that advertisers pay to have placed on news and entertainment websites. Oftentimes, the spots run before desired news and entertainment content.

Some companies are placing advertisements on MySpace to reach the coveted teen market. According to market research firm Grunwald Associates, 96 percent of tweens and teens use social networking sites like MySpace. The site was expected to bring in between $200 and $300 million in ad revenue in 2007. Marketers are committed to the site. In fact, when MySpace announced that it had discovered and closed down 29,000 user profiles that belonged to registered sex offenders, no companies dropped their advertising. *Advertising Age* reported the story with the headline "Advertisers Can't Afford to Quit MySpace."[6]

Companies are also running online ads on the personal pages of MySpace users. A study by MySpace owner Fox Interactive Media found that this form of advertising was particularly successful. When companies advertised on an individual's personal MySpace page, others who viewed the site recalled the brand better. Brand placement on MySpace pages strikes a chord with visitors because MySpace pages are so personal in nature. Therefore, any brand placed on an individual's MySpace page could be interpreted as an endorsement and/or an important part of the person's life. Rex Briggs from Marketing Evolution, the agency that performed the study, used Adidas as an example and said the placement is effective ". . . when I take the brand, put it on my profile page, and then all the [visitors] develop a deeper meaning for what Adidas stands for because of where it stands in my own personal story."[7]

Some companies are creating their own noncorporate websites, which attract a community of women worldwide. In many cases, the sites aren't meant to sell products directly, but are meant to allow women to interact with their brands in a casual, informational way. NBC Universal, which is owned by General Electric, owns iVillage, a splashy website full of tips and quizzes about beauty, motherhood, fitness, decorating, and entertainment. Procter & Gamble, which owns the Always and Tampax brands, created BeingGirl.com, a website that functions like a magazine for teens and tweens, with articles about fitness, relationships, shaving your legs, and, most important, menstruation. The pharmaceutical firm Roche Laboratories created a website called Flufacts.com, which includes tips on how to prevent the flu, entertaining content using the animated penguins from the film *Happy Feet,* and, of course, information about Roche's antiflu medication. In 2006, the cosmetics brand Maybelline created Whatispure.com to reach young women who spend time on web communities like MySpace and Facebook. Maybelline later closed down the site. When it was functioning, however, WhatIsPure.com did not show any Maybelline products. It was simply a collection of short questions floating across the screen in animated bubbles. The questions were girly and lighthearted, asking, "Blond or brunette?" and, "Heels or flip-flops?" After users answered a question, the bubble revealed how other people had voted, with current percentages. Maybelline's Director of Internet Kristen Yraola told *Adweek* magazine that women who go to WhatIsPure are typically young and comfortable with the web as a two-way medium. She said that Maybelline wanted girls and young women to spread the word to their friends.[8]

National television commercials are becoming an old-fashioned way of advertising, and their audience is eroding. In addition, the cost to produce commercials (an average of $400,000) is now seen as expensive by cost-conscious corporations who want a return on their investment. As one ad agency head told *The New York Times,* "In the '90s, it was about strategy. Now, it's only about money." In the same article, Carl Johnson, a longtime executive from traditional agencies, was of a similar opinion. Johnson, who started his own boutique agency, Anomaly, with a few other execs from traditional agencies, told the *Times,* "It's almost accepted that the model is broken and it's time for a new approach. No one comes to us for more of the same. Our last resort is an ad, if we can't think of anything else."[9]

Decades ago, agencies called the shots when it came to advertising. The client companies followed their advice. Today, companies are seizing back control and demanding that agencies give them a return on their investment and think beyond television commercials. They want diversification through online advertising, viral ads, and campaigns to generate coverage in the press and buzz among consumers.

While Baby Boomers are embracing technology and using the web in impressive numbers, teens and twentysomethings are still a few steps ahead with technology, using portable devices like never before. Cell phones, iPods, and PDAs (personal digital assistants) have never been more essential to these young consumers.

Christina, a twenty-two-year-old California hairdresser, said during my interview with her that her generation can adapt quickly to new technology, and that her friends are always anxiously awaiting the next tech gadget. "Everyone has the newest thing, and if technology changes, our generation is like, 'Okay, it's changed; let's move on now." Christina owns an iPod and a digital camera and has a Verizon cell phone that includes a small typewriter-style keypad, which allows her to text-message with ease. She text-messages much more often than she talks on the phone or uses email. Her phone also has "My Flix" on it, allowing her to record video messages and send them to friends. She's even heard about a new phone that has a video camera on the front, which allows users to look at the people they are talking to in real time. "It's like *The Jetsons,* where they had those compacts that would open to look at each other while talking on the phone. It's just like that. I can't wait for that to come out."

Advertisers are exploring ways to reach young consumers like Christina with these new portable devices. In 2006, companies spent about $900 million on ads that ran on cell phone screens, and one research firm estimates that by 2011, the market will grow to $11 billion in revenue.[10] Companies are creating their own ringtones and video content in hopes that consumers will download them to their cell phones, iPods, and computers. Bacardi, for example, has created its own Bacardi Mojito ringtone song. At Bacardimojito.com, users are invited to download the song to their cell phones, along with other videos and desktop images for their computers. The Bacardi website also includes a link to Bacardi B-Live Radio, an online service that allows customers to download DJ-engineered song mixes to their cell phones.

In 2005, Frito-Lay promoted some of its snacks, such as Doritos, though a text-message campaign. Consumers learned about the marketing campaign through mysterious billboards that asked them to text the letters "inNw" to a specific phone number, or visit a website called InNw.com. When consumers took the bait, they received text messages back, challenging them to guess what "inNw" meant.[11] They learned that it stands for "If not now, when?" The philosophical phrase "If not now, when?" was written by Hillel, a Talmudic scholar and rabbi, thousands of years ago—he also wrote, "If I am not for myself, who is for me? When I am for myself, what am I?" Frito-Lay believed the ancient phrase would resonate with younger consumers in Generation Y, whom the company calls Millennials.

In a press release from Frito-Lay, Lora DeVuono, vice president of advertising, said, "'if not now, when?' is all about living life in the now and taking advantage of every single opportunity possible. This attitude is what is important to Millennials, and it's how they look at the Doritos brand."

While the text-message approach made sense, the use of the ancient phrase seemed like a stretch to me. Most young consumers probably didn't know where the phrase originated. Those aware of it were likely offended that a corporation would use ancient writings to sell snack food. I found a few of those people posting their complaints online. One person wrote, "I won't eat Doritos ever again. . . . 'If not now, when?' . . . was not meant to sell tortilla chips."[12]

With respect to the text-messaging medium, DeVuono told *The New York Times,* "The inNw? campaign uses new, innovative approaches to reach consumers with this attitude in ways most relevant to them. . . . Text messaging and web fluency is spreading among consumers. In terms of lifestyle integration, it's the under-30 crowd that's focused on its complete integration in their lives."

Of the under-30 crowd, teenagers probably use text messaging most. According to a study by the Pew Internet & American Life Project, about half of U.S. teens have a cell phone, and 64 percent of those teens regularly send text messages through their cell phones. Therefore, while companies won't openly admit that they are targeting teens, text-messaging marketing initiatives allow companies to reach teens, oftentimes without parents' knowledge, since cell phones are such personal devices. Pew also found that teen girls text more than teen boys. One 2005 survey found that 57 percent of teen girls have sent a text message, compared with 40 percent of teen boys.[13]

Marketers are exploring other ways to reach tech-savvy girls and women through their cell phones. They are cognizant that consumers will reject ads on cell phones if the messages are too intrusive. Companies are exploring all of the options, experimenting, for example, with ways to run ads while a cell phone is downloading a new ringtone, or giving consumers free cell phone tools and services in exchange for viewing ads. A representative from Verizon Wireless told *The Seattle Times* that Verizon is conducting consumer trials, showing banner ads on cell phone screens. "We are taking the conservative approach," he said, adding that the company has been pleased with customer responses.

When consumers do turn to their old hangout, the television, a growing number of them are shielding themselves from advertising with the help of the digital video recorder (DVR), which is perhaps the greatest threat to the players of the advertising world. A DVR is like the protective older sibling who shields his little sister from the player's advances. DVRs hit the marketplace in the late nineties through the introduction of devices like TiVo allow television watchers to digitally record programs and then zip through the commercials of previously recorded programs. By the year 2000, TiVo was available in retail stores. Soon other manufacturers and cable providers rolled out their own digital recording devices. In 2005, about ten million American households owned digital video recorders, though various research firms estimate that by 2010, more than 40 million households will own digital video recorders.

The research firm Forrester is studying DVR use extensively, surveying consumers who own and use digital video recording devices. So far, it has reported that DVR consumers spend nearly 60 percent of their TV time watching recorded programs, in which they skip 92 percent of the commercials. This obviously has advertisers and television network executives worried. A 2006 study by Forrester and the Association of National Advertisers found that 78 percent of advertisers feel that traditional TV advertising has become less effective over the past two years. In compiling this report, Forrester surveyed 133 national advertisers representing about $20 billion in ad dollars. Those advertisers include Charles Schwab, Mattel, Johnson & Johnson, Verizon, and Pfizer. Nearly 70 percent of those surveyed said DVRs and video-on-demand services will reduce or eventually destroy the effectiveness of traditional thirty-second commercials. Nearly 60 percent of the advertisers surveyed said they would spend less on conventional television advertising when DVRs are in thirty million homes. Forrester believes DVRs will reach thirty million homes by 2009.[14]

In my estimation, about 50 percent of the women I spoke to owned

DVRs, and all of them spoke gleefully about the device's ability to skip past commercials. Thirtysomething Keisha, a single woman from Los Angeles, called TiVo "the greatest invention ever." Twentysomething DVR owner Katie, from Oregon, told me she doesn't miss commercials: "I don't feel like I'm missing anything, and when I go to the grocery store, it's not like I don't know what to buy now."

Because of the growing popularity of DVRs, there is more interest in spending the money to advertise during important live events, such as the Oscars, the Super Bowl, or the finale of *American Idol*. In the television world, these types of events are called "TiVo-proof," because even DVR owners are inclined to watch these programs live, thus eliminating their ability to zip through commercials.

The presence of DVRs has clouded the landscape for advertisers. Marketers aren't sure how many people are watching commercials and whether the prices of the ad buys are fair. More marketers are shifting dollars to the web, where there is more targeting and much more information about the number of people who view the ad. For example, marketers can post a quiz, ad, or video on a website and easily monitor how many viewers click it, how long they are engaged with it, and whether they email it to their friends. Mark Kaline, global media manager for the Ford Motor Company, told *The New York Times* that the web, in its ability to measure viewership so well, has raised the bar. "There are so many dollars involved in television and print and in other traditional media that we're looking for greater granularity to help with decisions."[15] By "granularity," Kaline meant that marketers need to know which mediums allow ads to best penetrate to the audience.

Knowing that a growing number of commercials are skipping past the eyeballs of American viewers, marketers asked Nielsen to measure the viewership of commercial breaks for television shows, instead of only measuring the viewership of television programs. Nielsen obliged. It is too soon to know how this will impact the way ad times are bought and sold. However, television networks are beginning to base their commercial slot pricing on the ratings of their commercial breaks, rather than the ratings of their programs. The television networks are now doing what they can to ensure good commercial-break ratings. They are scrambling to find other ways to keep viewers glued to the television set during breaks, which are also called "pods." Clearly, they are at a great disadvantage, since they don't create the content for commercials—ad firms and companies do. So networks are testing out "podbusters," which are usually ten- to twenty-second sketches slipped between ads in a commercial break. For example, during the comedy TV show *Scrubs,* NBC ran a podbuster that was simply a short interview with a cast member. In between commercials on Fox, the network ran sketches featuring an animated character named Oleg the Taxi Driver. Oleg was created specifically for Fox's podbuster content.

Marketing and media analyst Marissa Gluck, from the Los Angeles firm Radar Research, told me that she isn't sure these little slips of entertainment will be able to hold eyeballs and stop the fast-forward buttons on

DVR controllers. She believes the better solution is for Madison Avenue to create more entertaining commercials.

Since television is no longer the dominant media outlet, and since Americans are juggling hectic schedules with numerous media options, marketers are finding it more difficult to choose the best mediums for their ads. Since women make the majority of buying decisions, marketers are especially eager to pinpoint which media options women are choosing. One marketing group has learned more by segmenting women according to the media they like best and the times of day they consume media. The women's market consultancy Frank About Women believes that most women fall into one of four media-consumption categories. They include the Ultimate Infotasker, the Day Planner, the Environmental Homebody, and the Wired Adventurer.

Frank About Women's Executive Director Siobhan Olson defined Ultimate Infotaskers as those women who constantly expose themselves to media throughout their day, ping-ponging from one source to another. These women use TV, radio, blogs, and technological devices to access information, and they often know the news of the day, the hottest trends, and celebrity gossip before most of their friends and colleagues. Day Planners, on the other hand, consume media in a more organized fashion. Though they value media and want to be informed, they consistently visit the same media outlets each day at the same time. After they have visited their trusted sources, they generally ignore other media throughout their day. Environmental Homebodies consume mostly traditional media, keeping their televisions on all day, rarely venturing out of the home or to the web. These women have strong brand loyalties and aren't inclined to try a new product without being provoked through a trusted source within traditional media, such as seeing an ad during their favorite TV show or hearing that their favorite television show host uses the product. Wired Adventurers consume no traditional media, and instead use the web and remote devices, such as cell phones and PDAs to seek information. These women tend to be more brand adventurous and are more comfortable using technology.

Frank About Women has found that women who consume media similarly often have very different demographic backgrounds. For example, their research has found that upper-middle-class Baby Boomers (whom Frank About Women calls the Well-Feathered Empty Nesters) and middle-class moms (whom Frank About Women calls the Wal-Mart Moms) both consume media as Day Planners, though these two types of women differ in terms of their age and socioeconomics. Similarly, young college graduates (whom Frank About Women calls the Fun and Free Starters) and older single moms (whom Frank About Women calls the Successful Singles) both tend to consume media as Wired Adventurers. Therefore, when working with a client, Frank About Women uses this information as a tool to guide the distribution of its marketing messages. For example, Frank About Women would likely encourage a client to develop different ad messages for Well-Feathered Empty Nesters and Wal-Mart Moms, since these women likely wouldn't respond to the same content; however, the distribution strategy would likely be the same for these types of women, since both consume media as Day Planners.

Throughout my interviews, I found that each time marketers spoke about the future of their industry, they mentioned the Latino market. Due to immigration, rising education levels among Latinos, and the success of the Spanish-language media, Latinos' consumer power is surging. They represent the fastest-growing U.S. minority demographic: Nearly 50 million are believed to live in the United States. The Census Bureau projects that from 2000 to 2050, the Hispanic population will grow by 188 percent, to 102 million people. By comparison, the white non-Hispanic population is projected to grow by just 7 percent from 2000 to 2050, to 210 million people.[16] The Television Bureau of Advertising projected Latino buying power to be more than $900 billion in 2007.[17]

"You can't really argue with the demographics," marketing consultant Jennifer Woodard-Maderazo told me. "Immigration is huge, and it's not just the incoming market of new immigrants, but immigrants [who] have been around for twenty years, who have children—and that constitutes a bigger market." In describing the children of immigrants, *BusinessWeek* journalist David Kiley wrote, "Agencies view today's Latino explosion as similar to the Baby Boomer phenomenon in the postwar [United States], in which a generation of children who grew up with different mindsets from their more cautious parents became a driving force in a dynamic consumer period."[18]

Because of this rise in consumer power, companies are beginning to update their advertising approach to Latinos. In the past, most commercials and print ads aimed at this market reflected traditional stereotypes, showing large, close-knit families, and women cooking in the kitchen. But companies are beginning to create ads with more diverse themes.

Advertising firm Grupo Gallegos is leading the charge. Grupo Gallegos is often described by industry insiders as a "hot shop," having made a name for itself by creating award-winning, cutting-edge ads geared toward Latino consumers. I went to Grupo Gallegos to meet the people behind its fabulous reputation. There I spoke with Verena Sisa, director of planning and research. We talked about typical Latino-targeted ads that focus on traditional, clichéd portrayals, showing Latinos as being family-centric and watching soccer on television. Sisa called these "chips and salsa images," and told me that while there is a bit of truth to those conceptions, Latinos are looking for more updated messaging. On Univision and other Spanish-language networks, outdated commercials that show Grandma cooking in the kitchen and men watching soccer run one after another. Grupo Gallegos helps its clients break through that clutter, creating ads that are as funny and edgy as anything that runs during the Super Bowl.

For example, Grupo Gallegos revamped the California Milk Processor Board's campaign for milk by running quirky commercials that humorously exaggerate milk's ability to build strong bones and teeth. One commercial, called Teeth, shows a city of milk-drinking people whose teeth are so strong, they can eat through large objects and carry them around in their mouths.

In another commercial, called Amazing Contortionist, we meet a family of circus performers able to twist and bend to extremes thanks to milk's powers. The new campaign lifted sales, Sisa said.

This new strategy replaced a campaign marked by the slogan *"Familia, amor y leche"* ("Family, love and milk"). The old campaign was in direct contrast with the English-language campaign Got Milk?. Sisa explained that Latinos consume both English and Spanish media and probably noticed that the advertising in Spanish media didn't match what they saw in the mainstream. "Latinos don't live in a bubble," she said.

This is just one concern when marketing to this demographic. Marketers also need to consider that there are more than twenty different nationalities among Latinos. Wharton Management Professor Mauro Guillén told the school's business journal that this makes the Latino population in the United States extremely heterogeneous. Each nationality has different educational levels and degrees of buying power. "Cubans have the most financial resources and best skills, followed by Mexicans, Colombians, Ecuadorians, Central Americans, and, finally, the Puerto Ricans." In addition to financial distinctions, each nationality has different sensibilities, slang, and humor. Not surprisingly, a Peruvian or Cuban American consumer who viewed an ad with Mexican overtones would likely find the ad inauthentic. To help me understand better, Sisa asked me to imagine that I lived in another country and saw ads that always portrayed Americans as cowboys.

While companies should consider the ethnic nuances within the

Latino market, Sisa told me that it is nearly impossible for a company to develop tailored ads for each of the nationalities. Grupo Gallegos has found that Latinos of different nationalities have more in common with one another according to their level of acculturation. Those who are considered low-acculturated are more likely to be new to the United States, while those who are considered high-acculturated consume both English- and Spanish-language media and have been in the United States for a longer period of time. So, when working with a client, the first step is to determine which level of acculturation the client wants to reach, and what creative and distribution methods should be used to reach those consumers. The geographic region in the U.S. being targeted is also an important consideration, since Latinos in Miami, for example, have a different acculturation experience than those in, say, Nashville.

When the Dr. Pepper brand approached Grupo Gallegos, they wanted to reach low-acculturated consumers in Texas. Dr. Pepper happens to be a very popular drink in Texas, outselling Coca-Cola and Pepsi, Sisa said. So a Spanish-language billboard created by Grupo Gallegos read: YOU CAN SEE COWS, OIL, AND COWBOYS. BUT IF YOU DON'T SEE DR. PEPPER, YOU'RE NOT IN TEXAS. Dr. Pepper's overall slogan, which was used in ads targeted at all Latinos in Texas, was "The one we drink here."

Sisa told me that Grupo Gallegos aims to endear brands to Latinos, meaning that it doesn't want its clients' brands to just be names that Latinos know—they also must be brands they love. That involves truly knowing Latinos at the core. Grupo Gallegos pulls from the experiences and knowledge of its own staff, which is primarily Latino, including many first-generation Americans. The company also does its own research, going into the homes of Latinos to understand how they live and what they want. "When you want to make connections between brands and consumers, you need to understand who they are," Sisa said. "If you don't walk into their homes, if you don't hang out with their friends, you don't know."

Madison Avenue carries a number of misconceptions about Latino consumers, namely that they are low income. Research is refuting this idea. According to the Census Bureau, the median income among Hispanics was $30,735 in 2000.[19] By 2004, that number had climbed to $34,241.[20] A study from the research firm Ketchum found that Latinos contributed $450 billion to the U.S. economy in 2003. Ketchum also reported that 38 percent of Latinos surveyed considered themselves financially comfortable.

Financial power is likely one reason marketers have been slow to court the African American market with the same gusto with which they are courting the Hispanic market. While African American spending power has grown significantly over the past decade, it hasn't grown at the record-breaking numbers of the immigration-powered Hispanic market. In addition, marketers have assumed—incorrectly in some cases—that African American consumers spend less than white consumers. Slowly, research is proving these notions wrong. According to *Target Market,* which publishes an annual report called "The Buying Power of Black America," the buying power of the African American market in 1995 was estimated to be $325 billion; however, that number had surpassed $700 billion by 2005,[21] and is now believed to be near $1 trillion.[22] A 1997 *Black Enterprise* news story stated that black households spend more than white households on boys' clothing, athletic footwear, personal care services, and auto rentals. In that story, Norma Stanley, president of NFS, a communications consulting firm in Atlanta, responded to those statistics, saying, "If 12 percent of the population is using 40 percent of a product, corporations need to put at least that amount of their marketing budget toward this group. But that doesn't happen."[23]

African American leaders are generally frustrated that change isn't happening quickly enough. At a 2006 forum about diversity in advertising, the CEO of *Black Enterprise,* Earl "Butch" Graves, Jr., called the marketing/ advertising industry "one of the most racist industries in this country." Graves and other African American leaders called for more spending in minority media to attract black consumers. One argument from Madison Avenue is that ads in the general media reach African American consumers. However, Graves and others insist that more spending in minority media is necessary, and that companies should employ ad agencies and consultants who specialize in reaching African Americans, so that ads can be authentic, relevant, and tailored to black consumers.[24] The comments from Graves came as New York's Commission on Human Rights was investigating the absence of blacks in senior positions in the city's top ad firms. As a result of that 2006 investigation, the ad firms that were subpoenaed agreed to set goals for hiring more ethnically diverse employees.

Procter & Gamble is one company that has made an effort recently to reach African American consumers. In 2003, the corporation—which owns brands such as CoverGirl, Crest, and Tide—made a deeper commitment to the African American market by announcing that it would sponsor campaigns aimed at black consumers for a dozen of its large brands; it also announced that it would work with ad firms that specialize in reaching minority consumers.[25] Then, in 2007, the company launched My Black Is Beautiful, a campaign designed to incite discussion about how black women are portrayed in popular culture. The campaign was informed by research conducted by Procter & Gamble and *Essence* magazine, which found that 71 percent of African American women surveyed said that they are portrayed as worse than other racial groups in the media. Similarly to how Unilever ignited conversation about the definition of beauty through Dove's Campaign for Real Beauty, Procter & Gamble's My Black Is Beautiful campaign included a national tour, a trust fund, and more inspirational marketing for African American women.[26]

Procter & Gamble appears to be ahead of competitors when it comes to reaching its ethically diverse consumers. According to the advertising trade magazine *Advertising Age,* Procter & Gamble is the largest advertiser to the U.S. Latino market. P&G not only runs its own in-house Latino agency, Conill, but it also conducts copious research to understand this market. For example, through its own research, P&G learned that many Latinas felt alone in the United States, and that they craved recognition from their husbands and children. P&G's Tide brand integrated the research into commercials for Tide, which were targeted at Latina moms.

In one commercial, a husband and son notice how much work is being done around the house by their wife/mom, and they thank her. Leticia Dibildox, a marketing director for Proctor & Gamble's Hispanic division, told *Advertising Age* that after the spots aired on television, P&G received tearful, thankful calls from women on the company's toll-free line.

Maria, fifty-one and a mother from Burbank, California, remembered a commercial for P&G's Clairol Hydrience hair-color products featuring Dayanara Torres, a Puerto Rican beauty queen and the former wife of Marc Anthony. Maria appreciated seeing the ad and felt it represented positive opportunities for Latino people. Clairol signed Torres in 2006 to appear in its English- and Spanish-language advertising.

I asked a different Maria, twenty-seven and from Florida, what she thought of these ads. "I will say that when I see cosmetic companies or hair product companies that depict Hispanic celebrities or models, I think it's really cool," she said. "And it might even make me want to go, 'She probably has curly hair like me. This is someone who speaks my language and has the same culture as me,' and I think it's great that Dove or Pantene or the others are using, in mainstream media, Penélope Cruz or Salma Hayek. That elevates the role of Hispanic women. In that sense, it's pretty cool that you can identify with them."

But Maria isn't keeping tabs on the number of Latinos in advertisements and articles. "I don't know that I go home and say, 'Oh, they should have more Hispanic women in *Glamour*,'" she said. Maria is much more irritated by ethnic clichés in advertising. "It's like the whole Mexican hat thing, or, 'Let's put a chili somewhere in the ad.' It's very exaggerated, the idea that 'Well, we have to hit them over the head that this is a Latina woman.' We should be past that point," she said.

Eighteen-year-old Jamie, a college student in the Chicago area, epitomizes the market of the future: She is a young Latina who frequents the web and owns various technological devices. Jamie is of Mexican, Danish, and German descent, though she identifies most with her Mexican heritage. "I'm very proud of my nationality," she told me, explaining that her family relationships are very strong, in part because of Mexican customs. Jamie told me that she knows previous generations of her family struggled, but she sees a bright future for herself as she makes her way through her first year of college.

Jamie doesn't see many Latino people and themes in the ads she encounters, and she wishes she saw more. I asked her what she would think if she did see an ad that was obviously meant to reach Latino consumers, or even showed a person who looked like her. "It might grab my attention more because it is my culture, my heritage. I would be like, 'Oh, wow, look at that, instead of, 'Oh, just another white girl in advertising.'"

Like many her age, Jamie is plugged in with numerous technological gadgets. Her most prized possessions are her 30-gig iPod—which has six thousand songs on it—her laptop computer, her digital camera, and her cell phone. She told me that she bought all of these tech gadgets with her own money. She spends a couple of hours each day on the web, visiting social networking sites MySpace and Facebook daily. She rarely watches television. "I don't notice online ads. I'm so used to the Internet that I just avoid them," she said.

I tell her about the future of advertising—how she could soon see ads splashed across her cell phone screen. "I wouldn't like that at all," she told me. "I think cell phones are for communication purposes and not to try to get you to purchase something. I don't use it to buy things. I use it to reach my [family] or figure out where someone [at school] is." The same applies to her iPod. She uses it when she is relaxing or working out. She said an ad's rightful place is in a magazine, on television, or on the web. Ads on her personal devices are too intrusive.

While Latinos make up an enormous segment of consumers, there are other powerful groups that the players of the ad world are spending new dollars to reach. Women's marketing expert and author Andrea Learned spent more than seventeen years in the marketing industry and now consults and writes on marketing topics. She believes that the number of single people—specifically, single women—will grow tremendously in the future, and that marketers are just beginning to cater to the needs and desires of single women. This belief is based on a number of statistics showing that single women are one of the fastest-growing segments of the population. Learned pointed to research from pollsters Kellyanne Conway and Celinda Lake, who run their own research firms and cowrote the book *What Women Really Want.* According to Conway and Lake, more than twenty-two million American women live alone, an 87 percent increase in the past two decades. This accounts for one-third of all American women.[27] After analyzing the most recent census figures, *The New York Times* found that in 2005, 51 percent of women said they were living without a spouse, up from 35 percent in 1950 and 49 percent in 2000.[28] Lake and Conway believe that, for the first time in history, unmarried women as a demographic have a significant influence on the culture.

Learned believes that, so far, marketers haven't responded to this shift with enough vigor. When marketers and corporate executives turned their attention to women, they first went to moms. That was the more obvious choice, but it left out a huge number of single women. "If [marketers] just started talking to their customers, they would see that they have single women, and a lot of them don't have to depend on other people to make the purchase decisions." Learned explained that when a company decides to reach single women, it often defaults to an image taken from the HBO show *Sex and the City*. Images of single women in ads show them as wild girls in metropolitan settings, sipping cosmopolitans until 3:00 AM and donning designer clothing. "They're missing a huge chunk of single women," Learned said. "*Sex and the City* is already dated. People don't live like that."

Thirty-year-old Stacey, who's single and from Los Angeles, agreed. "The ads are all about looking really great and owning all of this really great stuff. You don't want to be single and not own a really great purse. I've always felt like the ads present being single as so glamorous, and you want that life, but that isn't the reality for most twenty- and thirtysomethings. Most [women] starting out have a crappy apartment. They don't have the money for the latest designer bags. It's hard to live up to the image of a single woman. [Advertisers] don't understand what it is really like."

One single-woman stereotype that annoys twenty-six-year-old Katie, from Oregon, is, "Because you're single and you don't have anyone to cook for, all you want is a frozen dinner. You don't want to cook like a regular person. You want something out of a box. That irritates me."

Learned said marketers also incorrectly assume that single women desperately want to be married. Take, for example, a commercial for the referral service 1-800-DENTIST, where a woman calls the 1-800-DENTIST operator and tells her, "I'm recently divorced and I'm looking to spend some money on a little self-improvement." After the operator offers to help her find a dentist, the woman says, "Can you find me a husband, too?" In response, Learned said, "[Single women] are not sitting in a corner, worried that they are single. They are generally quite happy. . . . The myth that there is just one thing that motivates your life—and that is a partner—it absolutely isn't the case now. Women who get divorced are like, 'Fine.' They are happy to not get remarried ever again."

Marketing expert Holly Buchanan said that most often, ads aimed at Baby Boomers and retirees show a man and woman vacationing together. "There's a happy couple dancing or playing golf or bridge. But the stats show that women are marrying men older than them and outliving them, and there is a huge number of divorced and widowed women living life alone." Buchanan says she rarely sees a commercial that reflects this reality. She was glad to see an exception: a commercial for Lincoln Financial Group. It shows a woman in her late fifties or early sixties in varied circumstances—in a rocking chair on the porch, in a village in Africa helping kids, and on the beach, staring out at the waves.

Buchanan said she talked to the agency that created the ads, and found that the staff had done their own research about Baby Boomer women before creating the ad. "I think this is a combination of a company going in the right direction and a creative agency willing to craft that message," she said.

Learned explained that some marketers incorrectly assume that single women don't make enough money to afford major purchases, and that companies therefore devote fewer marketing dollars their way. She also believes that, for the same reason, single women are treated differently in sales situations—something she has experienced firsthand. Real estate agents have steered her toward condos, as opposed to houses. She's even caught car salesmen looking over her shoulder to see where her husband is.

However, statistics show that single women have significant funds and are not waiting for husbands to make major buying decisions. They are buying cars, homes, and vacations, and many women are taking those vacations solo, Learned said, adding, "They aren't waiting for big groups of people to do things with them."

Thirty-one-year-old Taguhi, a graduate student from Indiana, is a perfect example of the single woman Learned described. She has already purchased two homes and has paid for a solo road trip across the country, followed by a monthlong European vacation. "I was tired of, 'Oh, this person can't take eight weeks off' or, 'Oh, that person doesn't have the money,'" she said. "I wanted to see those things, and I couldn't wait anymore. However hard it was to be by myself, it was still worth it in the end, because now I can say I've been to Rome." Taguhi's home purchases have further boosted her confidence. "It's not like, 'Oh, I need a man to tell me what that big word 'escrow' is,'" she said with a laugh. Her single status wasn't an issue when she bought her homes, possibly because her agents were also women. But it was a different story when she bought her car and some other larger purchases. "They can see you coming a mile away. They are definitely looking to take advantage of you because you don't have the man with you. And if it's a store, they think that you aren't going to spend a lot of money, so they concentrate their attention somewhere else."

This is where marketers can refocus and win the hearts of single woman, Learned said. "Single women, because of their situation, are more blown away when [a company] gets it," she said. "They'll be saying, 'Oh my gosh, that brand really *gets* that I'm not going to be asking my husband to buy this'." When single women notice, albeit in amazement, that a company is making the effort to reach them, they are more inclined to become an evangelist for that company, spreading the word to their friends. And single women also have outstanding networks of friends to spread the positive word-of-mouth. Case in point: Single woman Maria, twenty-seven, from Miami, told me that she and a single female coworker were recently talking about the DeBeers right-hand-ring advertising campaign. Known for its "A diamond is forever" slogan, DeBeers aimed a new message at single women over thirty-five, telling them that they could buy a diamond ring for themselves and proudly wear it on their right hand. "It's saying, 'You can take care of yourself and get yourself a great rock,'" Maria said. "That appeals to the side of me that says, 'You are independent; you can do your own thing.'"

In addition to Hispanics and single women, companies are beginning to recognize the buying power of gay, lesbian, bisexual, and transgender consumers. Between 7 and 10 percent of the U.S. population is estimated to be gay or lesbian, and research shows that these consumers have more dispensable income than the national average. According to a reader survey conducted by Harris Interactive on behalf of the National Gay Newspaper Guild, the surveyed gays and lesbians had more than twice as many college degrees as the average U.S. adult (67 percent, as opposed to 25 percent). They were more than two times as likely to have an individual income over $50,000 (43 percent, as opposed to 21 percent) and almost two times as likely to have a net worth over $500,000 (26 percent, as opposed to 14 percent). That study revealed that gay and lesbian consumers are more likely to be early adopters of technology, belong to a health club, travel abroad, dine out, and visit museums and theaters.[29]

"The gay market is not as big as the Latino market, but the data is compelling," marketing consultant Jennifer Woodard-Maderazo told me. "In spirits, technology, travel, entertainment, and automotive, gay people spend more." While American society has progressed in its acceptance of the gay community, these consumers have been largely untapped by corporate America, despite the research that shows the tremendous spending power they have. That is one reason the global communications firm Fleishman-Hillard created FH Out Front, a practice group devoted to helping companies and organizations reach the GLBT (gay/lesbian/bisexual/transgender) market through public relations and marketing campaigns. I spoke with the cochairs of FH Out Front, Ben Finzel and Steve Kauffman, senior vice president and vice president, respectively. Fleishman-Hillard projected the 2007 consumer buying power of the GLBT market to be $690 billion. That number is expected to grow to an estimated $835 billion by 2011. "That is a huge amount of expendable income," Finzel said. "It's a great starting place to put the gay/lesbian community in perspective."

Still, few companies are marketing openly and directly toward GLBT consumers and are showing positive GLBT portrayals in traditional advertising. For example, Amélie Mauresmo—who held the number-one spot in women's tennis for much of 2006 and is openly gay—has far fewer endorsements than many other female tennis stars. In a more extreme example from the past, tennis star Billie Jean King lost all her endorsements in 1981 after a lawsuit revealed that she was gay.

The vast majority of companies that are reaching gay consumers advertise on gay websites, the Logo cable network (which runs gay-themed television programming), and gay magazines such as *The Advocate*. Therefore, gay-targeted advertising is less visible to straight customers. In the mainstream, some companies appear to be tiptoeing into this market through ads that show two people of the same sex together, though their relationship is unclear. Ads like this are sometimes referred to as "gay vague," a term coined by Michael Wilke, a journalist who now runs the organization Commercial Closet.

Woodard-Maderazo recalled seeing a gay vague ad in a Target store in February 2007. "I saw a poster of two women hugging, and it was related to Valentine's Day," she told me. "They put two pretty girls together. Are they lesbians? Are they sisters? It appeals to the gay market but doesn't offend anyone. It's ambiguous." Similarly, in the late '90s, Abercrombie & Fitch print ads appeared in the company's magazine/catalog showing young men standing together in their underwear. In 2001, a print ad for Beefeater gin showed two women standing together seductively. That ad ran in both mainstream magazines and gay media.

Thirty-one-year-old lesbian Nicole, from Denver, told me she was not bothered by gay vague advertising, though she would much prefer companies to openly market to her as a lesbian. She does not expect this kind of boldness from corporations. "I would be very surprised, because I know they may be opening a door that might actually cause them to lose [dominant] culture support."

A few major corporations do openly advertise and market to gay and lesbian consumers in mainstream media. In 1997, the automaker Subaru began actively marketing to lesbians after conducting its own research, which revealed that lesbians were fans of the automobiles. One print ad from 2000 spoke of the car, and probably its lesbian consumers, with the line "It's not a choice. It's the way we're built." A similar print ad showed an SUV careening down a hill, along with the line "Entirely comfortable with its orientation." Subaru also hired Martina Navratilova and several other female athletes to star in its ads in 2000.[30]

International furniture retailer IKEA has portrayed nontraditional families in its advertising in the American mainstream media numerous times since the '90s. Another commercial, which ran on several mainstream cable networks in 2006, showed a gay male couple in their living room with their daughter. The narrator said, "Why shouldn't sofas come in flavors, just like families?"[31]

American Express has marketed to gay and lesbian consumers since the mid '90s and has been praised by the gay and lesbian nonprofit group the Human Rights Campaign for running ads that depict them in authentic and respectful ways. In 1999, the company ran a print ad in mainstream magazines that promoted its Small Business Services credit card. The ad showed a male couple who started their own dog-biscuit bakery in Missouri.[32]

In 2007, Levi's released a commercial with two different endings. In the mainstream media, the guy in the commercial is shown getting his girl. The same Levi's commercial that ran on the gay television network Logo ended with the guy getting his guy. Levi's Vice President of Marketing Robert Cameron told *Advertising Age* that the company was faced with a tight budget and couldn't afford to create two completely different commercials. Company executives debated if it was fair to create an ad with different endings, rather than spending more and creating a dedicated commercial especially for the gay market with lower production value. "But [then] we thought, *If we're going to do an ad for them, they deserve the same production values.* . . . So doing the same commercial with different endings seemed to us to be a message about absolute equality," Cameron said. Logo President Brian Graden called Levi's a progressive company that comes from "a very credible place." He added, "We think [speaking to the gay audience specifically] is a smart way for marketers to go. We have research that shows our audience has a much greater affinity for advertisers on Logo that have made a conscious decision to reach them."[33]

According to the Human Rights Campaign, American Express is one of the few companies that has invested substantial sums of money in its own consumer research about gay and lesbian consumers. The company spent $250,000 alone in 1997.[33] But overall, the business world does little marketing research on gays and lesbians. The research that is available has not studied lesbians and gay men separately.

"So what people are left with are stereotypes or gut instincts," Wilke said. The common excuse for this lack of research is the cost, though companies comfortably spend hundreds of thousands of dollars to research other segments of consumers. The business world is simply less committed to this market, and when most companies do decide to take a step toward marketing to the gay community, their plans aren't necessarily long-term. "Very few end up hanging around for more than a year or so," Wilke said.

Much of the research on gay and lesbian consumers exists because the National Gay Newspaper Guild has funded studies. The NGNG began funding research in 1988, when several gay newspapers pooled their resources to hire a reputable research firm to survey their readers. This provided some of the earliest consumer statistics on gay and lesbian consumers in the United States. Over the years, the NGNG has continued its research, which has informed companies of the consumer buying power of the gay and lesbian market. It has sparked other firms to conduct their own research on this market, and it has led to more marketing aimed at gays and lesbians, which will only continue to grow.

Gay consumers notice the companies that make a genuine effort to reach them, Finzel and Kauffman said. "One of the key ways that gay, lesbian, bisexual, and transgender people learn about products is from one another. Word of mouth is huge in the sense that we all talk to each other and we share information, virtually, over the Internet, on websites and blogs, at bars, with our friends," Finzel told me. "This is a real key way and leveragable asset for companies that tap into that." Halfhearted attempts stand out and insult gay consumers. For example, Finzel and Kauffman explained that some companies run the same heterosexual-themed ads in gay media that were made for mainstream media, such as one that showed a man giving a woman a piece of jewelry, and another, for a car company, that showed a man and woman driving together.

"This is a really skeptical audience, and we look to see if you are walking the talk or trying to take advantage of us by doing one little thing," Finzel told me. "We want you to be an active participant in our community in supporting us, and not just looking to us as a consumer base." Gay and lesbian consumers check to see whether companies are developing gay-friendly policies for their employees, such as benefits for same-sex partners and nondiscrimination policies, or whether they are supporting gay and lesbian organizations and participating in events attended by that community. Gay consumers are also known to access the websites of watchdog organizations, such as the Human Rights Campaign, which monitors companies and ranks them according to their gay-friendly policies and actions.

Nicole drives a Subaru, although she told me that she didn't necessarily buy it because of the brand's advertising for the lesbian community, or because Subaru has worked with the National Center for Lesbian Rights (NCLR). Her uncle recommended the car. "I don't think the NCLR thing would have mattered if they didn't have the product I wanted." Overall, Nicole would most like advertisers to show less traditional families and not perpetuate what she calls the "hetero-normative." She told me that advertising tries to appeal to mainstream society, but that that "doesn't represent the true society we have. . . . I would like to see just more of everything, seeing all different kinds of families, not just one socially imposed norm."

It was much simpler for the players of the advertising world back in the '50s. Then, the majority of women were stay-at-home moms who watched a handful of television shows as their prime means of entertainment. Over the last fifty years, everything has scattered. Women are creating new identities for themselves and aren't limited by their age, job, or family structure. They are enjoying entertainment on hundreds of channels, TiVo, the web, cell phones, and iPods. There are new markets that require companies to go the extra mile to reach them. If the player wants to remain relevant, he has to be able to find them and be courageous enough to forge into new markets. But even after a company locates its target consumer, there is still much more work ahead. The company's marketing and/or advertisements must still grasp the consumer's attention, charm her, and convince her to buy. In today's hectic world, perhaps the most difficult of those tasks is commanding her attention—this is discussed in the next chapter.

CHAPTER 5

The Show-off

The show-off thrives on attention. His bravado makes some laugh and others cringe. While he may offend more people than he charms, the fact remains that everyone knows who he is.

In today's overcrowded marketing landscape, attention is half the battle. "People are so bombarded with 'interruption marketing,'" said Holly Buchanan, who writes the blog Marketing to Women Online. "They are doing everything they can to tune it out, whether it's spam blockers or pop-up blockers or TiVo." The bombardment of advertising is perhaps best illustrated in dollar amounts. Companies spend millions of dollars on marketing campaigns—usually about 10 percent of their gross revenue each year. According to TNS Media Intelligence, total ad spending in 2006 was nearly $150 billion. TNS estimated that ad spending would grow by 1.7 percent, to $152.3 billion, in 2007.[1] The top ten advertisers spent more than $18 billion on their marketing pursuits in 2006. The biggest spenders were Procter & Gamble and General Motors, which each spent about $3 billion.

A 2006 study by research consultants Blackfriars Communications projected that U.S. companies would spend $615 billion on marketing as a whole during the year. Blackfriars said that if marketing were an actual industry, it would be the ninth largest in the United States, larger than the country's entire media industry. After spending this money, company executives want to see that their ad dollars are paying off, making a positive impression on today's female consumers. But the argument can be made that ad overload has done just the opposite.

The marketplace has been flooded with ad clutter, which has made it difficult for ads to break through. "We've gone from a selling mode to [an] engaging mode," women's marketing consultant and author Marylou Quinlan said. "If you're a savvy 40-plus consumer, you've seen more ads than you care to remember," she said, adding that it's just as difficult to reach savvy, skeptical young people. "So you've got to chase that consumer and bring them in."

Advertising Age columnist Bob Garfield explained that young people, particularly those in Generation Y, aren't playing by the same time-honored rules of media and advertising. "There has long been this silent quid pro quo of, *You give us content for free; we'll watch your commercials.* That is changing." This means that Gen Yers are not giving in, forcing advertisers to cave and meet them more than halfway. "[Young people] claim to hate ads and marketing. They think it sullies whatever media environment it enters, but they are willing to live with brand messages if the ad is cool in its own right," Garfield told me. "It has to have value as content, and if it does, they'll accept the embedded [advertising] message."

Garfield described the new method, as "Let the joke get ahead of the product." He was quick to note that this has long been considered a flawed advertising method. But now, he said, "That's what you have to do. That's an issue and one of the great challenges that marketers face." As a result, marketers are talking less about their products during commercials, and are instead producing entertaining, funny spots that look more like thirty-second films.

Marketing veteran Steve Hall said product information is also secondary because of the abundance of information available online. "It used to be that you would talk about the product in an advertisement. But now, all that information is on the web. So many marketers believe all we need to do is get the person's attention," Hall said.

Marylou Quinlan said that "the growing tide of TiVo is forcing advertisers to find ways to stop that crazed finger on the TiVo [controller]. You find that [the consumer] might stop if the ad is funny, as opposed to serious. The advertisers are in a whatever-it-takes philosophy."

One of the key talents of the show-off is comedy. Marketing consultants and coauthors Andrea Learned and Lisa Johnson agree that humor is a powerful tool in reaching a female audience, because women often find humor in common experiences. When a marketer can make a woman laugh by showing a relatable experience, it shows her that the brand really "gets her." In an effort to produce humorous, relatable characters and situations, marketers seek the help of professional comedians—both stand-up comedians and comedy troupe players—to inspire, write, and star in their ads. Comedy writer Demetri Martin was hired to star in a Microsoft Vista online campaign. *Daily Show* contributor and comedian John Hodgman is known for playing the PC in the Mac commercials. Comedians Peter Grosz and T. J. Jagodowski star in the Sonic commercials. These are just three of many examples. I called the famed Second City comedy troupe in Chicago to ask if their comedians are occasionally hired by ad firms to write and star in ads. The woman who answered the phone at Second City confirmed that this was true, but wouldn't elaborate, and took a message for a Second City spokesperson, who never called me back.

Humor is also being used more prevalently by Republican and Democratic candidates in political ads, rather than typical attack ads or "where I stand" ads. Hillary Clinton spoofed the finale of *The Sopranos,* by showing her and her husband eating onion rings in a diner. Governor Bill Richardson kicked off his campaign with humorous commercials as well. Richardson's campaign spokesman, Pahl Shipley, told *Advertising Age,* "We understand that we are an insurgent candidate and had to do something to stand out from the white noise of political advertising. It was a way to stand out, to stand apart, but with a serious message of: 'Give him a look before you make up your mind.'"[2]

One of the other ways to get the attention of consumers is to produce humorous commercials that offend some people and get everyone talking, in hopes that the buzz will lead to sales. One of the most memorable examples came in 1995, when Clairol resurrected its Herbal Essences brand with a series of provocative commercials that showed a woman in the shower, moaning delightfully, as if the shampoo was leading her to orgasm. Clairol took cues from the beloved scene in the comedy flick *When Harry Met Sally,* where Meg Ryan's character fakes an orgasm in a restaurant. The ad broke through the ad clutter, yielded a handful of news stories, and produced big sales, going from near obscurity to becoming the number two shampoo and conditioner in its category, behind Pantene.[3]

Clairol's Senior Product Manager Jane Owen admitted that the commercials "made Clairol's own employees gulp" when they saw them for the first time, and that Clairol received a few complaint calls. But overall, the commercials were strong enough for women to remember them (Owen called it "a high recall level"), turning Herbal Essences into a hit, especially with teens and early twentysomethings.[4] As a testament to how the culture has changed, this ad was very controversial when it came out, but it probably wouldn't raise too many eyebrows today.

Haircare companies still emulate the provocative character of the Herbal Essences campaign, using irreverence to break through the clutter. In 2006, Sunsilk rolled out its Get Hairapy marketing campaign with commercials featuring Mario Cantone, a gay comedian best known for his supporting role on *Sex and the City*. On the show, Cantone played a gay man who mercilessly told the women exactly what he thought about their horrible outfits, boring parties, and questionable boyfriends. His voice in the Sunsilk commercials tells women that their hair needs help. Sunsilk's print ads, which I saw in *InStyle* magazine, did not feature Cantone but captured his frankness and included statements such as, "My hair is as flat as my boyfriend after a few drinks," and, "My hair is so frizzy I should give it a Brazilian." The print ads were provocative and spunky enough to make young women listen, and were rooted in the honesty of the gay man, Quinlan said, adding, "There's been a huge love affair between women and gay men when it comes to women and beauty."

Even more mundane products aimed at women have gotten an advertising tune-up, using humor to push the envelope a bit. For example, Pepto-Bismol's recent campaign shows a group of men rapping the company's theme song, which is "Nausea, heartburn, indigestion, upset stomach, diarrhea." As the rappers dance, they coordinate gestures to each of the words, even motioning toward their backsides when rapping the word "diarrhea." Initially I thought the commercial was targeted at men, but then I began seeing the commercial run frequently during my favorite Food Network program. Not surprisingly, Pepto-Bismol's Brand Manager Karen Klei told *USA Today* that the company used the wacky commercials to "be engaging and break through the clutter."[5]

While most commercials for pregnancy tests feature a soft-spoken woman who speaks discreetly about "a woman's need to know," a 2006 commercial for the Clearblue Easy Digital Pregnancy Test took a completely different approach. The ad mockingly used an announcer, *Star Trek*–like music, and staging that harkened back to the sci-fi film *2001:*

A Space Odyssey to humorously highlight the technological advances of the digital test. The commercial shows a close-up of the testing stick and a stream of liquid hitting it in slow motion, while the announcer says in an exaggerated voice, "It has arrived. The next generation of pregnancy tests. Introducing the most sophisticated piece of technology you will ever pee on." After the ad went public, Doug Cameron, founding partner of the firm Amalgamated, which created the ad, told *Adweek* magazine that the goal was to turn Clearblue Easy into a cultural icon in the women's reproductive health market. He said, "Our competitors [such as EPT and First Response] are saying, without saying, that on some level . . . these things can only be discussed using ladylike euphemisms. Internally we were calling [our product] the pregnancy test for the *Sex and the City* generation."[6]

The ad didn't sit well with the women I talked to. Thirtysomething Miranda, a big fan of *Sex and the City,* said, "It's odd. It seems disjointed and misplaced. There are all these references to technology and digital performance, and even the font is very *Star Trek,* or something that seems a far departure from what women are really concerned with at the time they might be buying this sort of product. The peeing thing is disturbing, too. I really, really don't like that. I also don't care to hear a man's voice presented this way. It's farcical, but not funny enough to pull it off." Twentysomething Jackie, from Boston, said, "I have seen that ad, and it doesn't make me want to use that particular pregnancy test at all. I like pregnancy test ads where they show the couple waiting together. I don't like thinking about the particulars of peeing on a stick when I think about finding out whether or not I am pregnant. Also, speaking as a pregnant woman currently, I took at least two tests before I really started telling people I was pregnant. That's just how I am. I will always double-check anything I buy over the counter and take in my own home. So advertising [based] solely on the accuracy of the test does nothing for me, because I am going to take it again, no matter what."

Clorox also traded traditional ad content for "edgy and bizarre" in a series of commercials for its Tilex, Pine-Sol, and Liquid-Plumr products—and saw an increase in sales.[7] Household cleaners have long been advertised the old-fashioned way: with the crazed mom and her sparkling-clean porcelain sinks. But Clorox—under the guidance of marketing firm DDB Worldwide in San Francisco—stepped out of the box with ads that were quirky and weird. In one string of ads, some peculiar characters show that they are in denial about the mold in their homes. Each commercial is capped off with their shrieking, "No!" at the horror of the grime.

Tarang Amin, a vice president of marketing for Clorox, spoke to *Advertising Age* about the commercials in 2006, telling them, "As much as I love [DDB's creative] work, reacting to it as a businessperson, I love that our advertising effectiveness in 2004 went up 30 percent and in 2005 went up 37 percent." I wanted to speak to Mr. Amin about the effectiveness of the campaign, but his press representative never returned my messages. *Advertising Age,* which was apparently cool enough to elicit a conversation with the nouveau-hip Clorox, reported that the company's bleach, bathroom cleaners, and trash bags all saw shares rise following the new ad campaigns.

A 2005 Got Milk? commercial showed frantic, sweaty men stampeding the supermarket to buy countless gallons of milk. At the dairy case, two men were shown fighting over the last carton. Another man was seen raiding a milkman's truck. Finally, a voice gave the punch line: "Recent studies have shown that calcium reduces the effects of PMS." The commercial ended with a man walking through the door of his home, carrying a grocery bag stuffed with milk cartons and a long-stemmed rose. He fearfully said, "Honey, I'm home."

I will admit, with the music and editing, the commercial was produced cleverly, and I did think it was funny. But then came a bad aftertaste. I wondered, *Is my PMS really something to joke about? Do the folks at the milk board really think women are monsters whose husbands will try anything to tame us?* The milk humor was likely designed to appeal to a younger audience that wouldn't take offense at such a joke.

When I asked a few twentysomething women what they thought of the commercial, the resounding answer was, "It's funny" and, "What's the big deal?" Thirtysomething wife Andrea, from Phoenix, sent me an email about the commercial. In the subject line, she wrote, "the best commercial ever." But fortysomething Kay, from Kansas City, took offense to the commercial, describing it as degrading to women. Kay is no feminist. In fact, during the height of the feminist movement (when Kay was graduating from high school), she willingly skipped college to become a stay-at-home wife and mother, despite the urging of her teachers and counselors. Kay told me that life experience has made her more defensive about gender stereotypes and the humor that is thrown around in advertising. She said, "In my marriage of twenty-two years, I would sometimes get frustrated by my husband's actions. His response would sometimes be that I must be menstruating. I would have a rational, intelligent concern, and it would be turned into an emotional disagreement." Kay told me that young women haven't had the experience of not being taken seriously, and because of that, they don't realize that throughout their lives, they may not get the same respect men get in the workforce and in the family. That has been the reality for her, and she believes this injustice continues today. She added, "Young women are still idealistic, which is a good thing in most situations. But since the men in the commercial look a little older and look like they have been in a relationship for a while, the younger women might not see themselves in the commercial, and thus are able to laugh at an older generation."

Kay's point sheds light on why most of the 40-plus women I spoke to were critical of ads that joke about the differences between men and women, and why women under 40 were less bothered by them. Young women were far less critical of all of the edgy, sexual, and sexist jokes in advertising. It is unknown whether that is due to today's desensitized, fast-paced media environment, or whether it's simply a matter of being young, as Kay suggested.

A 2005 Gallup Poll found that Americans disagree about what is moral depending on their age. Nearly half (47 percent) of the youngest adults surveyed—those aged 18 to 29—said they were satisfied with the moral and ethical climate in America, while only a third (32 percent) of adults aged 65 and older said they were satisfied. Gallup has asked this morality question of these age groups annually since 2001, and has found similar results each year.

At the same time, it is undeniable that today's media and entertainment environment has exposed young women to more crude, violent, sophomoric content in their impressionable years than previous generations have seen. These are the women who first idolized Britney Spears and Christina Aguilera as tweens; these women watched the pop stars go through their innocent and dirty phases, and then they replaced their teen idols with Carrie Bradshaw from HBO's *Sex and the City*. A search on MySpace for "Sex and the City" returned more than three-hundred-thousand hits. Many of those hits were for the MySpace pages of twenty-somethings who listed the show as one of their favorites. These are the young women who mimic the characters from *South Park*, listen to Howard Stern on satellite radio, and discuss who's doing who on *The Real World*. The college girls shown in *Girls Gone Wild* are part of this generation. These are the women who wear Abercrombie & Fitch T-shirts that bear risqué phrases on their chests, such as "Who needs brains when you have these?" and "Bitchy is my middle name." They have not known a time in their lives apart from the everything-goes magnetism of the web and reality television, making them even more likely to discuss nearly anything in the open—PMS, biological clocks, Brazilian waxes, bathroom habits, and their sex lives.

Twenty-five-year-old Heidi is part of this generation. She is a first-grade teacher. Her young skin looks healthy and rosy without the help of any makeup. She dresses in preppy sweater sets and khakis and speaks in the perfect teacher voice. Heidi lives in ultraconservative Salt Lake City, and she is one of the relatively few liberal non-Mormons there. She openly plays the part of the rebel, exposing her liberal views about almost everything: economics, gay marriage, Iraq, poverty, gun control, you name it. She's often met with horrified looks or disappointed stares from coworkers, such as the time she suggested that the teachers at her school not celebrate Columbus Day until after telling their students about the many atrocities Columbus committed. Heidi revels in her freedom and in the edge she exudes that is shocking to others. In the same way that Heidi is more liberal than most others in her community, people in Heidi's age group generally live with a looser set of boundaries than people from previous generations.

It didn't surprise me to hear that Heidi and her friends enjoy beer commercials and aren't offended by blond jokes, fart jokes, or condom ads. She took no issue with any of the ads I showed her. She told me she just isn't easily offended by anything. "Blond jokes and jokes that portray females as stupid don't offend me because I'm secure in who I am. As far as *South Park* and rude humor, I think there was an allure to that when I was younger because, you know, [our] parents didn't like it. Because they would shake their heads when [MTV cartoon characters] Beavis and Butthead were frying rats in the deep fryer or making jokes about going the bathroom. It was kind of exciting."

I got a similar reaction from twenty-seven-year-old Tesia. When I asked her which commercials she could remember, she first pointed to one that she admitted was crude. "Some people might think this is crass, but I liked this one where the guy picks up his date. He walks up, opens the car door. And as he is walking around to the other side, she passes gas in the car really loudly, thinking that she is being discreet. And then he says, 'Have you met my family in the backseat?' and the [people] in the backseat [say], 'Oh, we've already met,'" Tesia said, giggling. That commercial, for the pager company SmartBeep, ran sometime in 1999 or 2000 but has lived on through the web. The video of the commercial is posted on slews of websites because many people still think it's funny. Tesia believes this kind of ad appeals to women as much as it does to men. "We are so overexposed that we don't get offended anymore. I was born and raised in the '80s, and the '80s was a time of overindulgence," she said. "I just remember it being 'entertainment at whatever cost.' I think that's part of it. So things that I think are funny are things my mom wouldn't get."

Twenty-two-year-old hairdresser Christina, who lives in a Southern California suburb, said, "I don't think I have one friend who would be offended by a blond joke or any kind of generalization," she said. "And it's not just hairdresser friends. I have friends in college who are the same." I asked her if she felt the same way about rude humor, such as content from Howard Stern, vulgar jokes, and locker room talk. "I don't care. I'm not offended by it. I think [young women] are just numb to it. We've heard it from, like, fifth grade. Guys will talk about [oral sex] right in front of us. It's not offensive. And I think that goes for men, too, because I can talk about tampons in front of my guy friends. More girls burp and fart in front of guys now. Women have learned to be more vulgar. And it's like that Carl's Jr. [Paris Hilton] commercial. I'm fine with it, but I would be very uncomfortable watching that with my boyfriend's dad, or his mom. She actually freaked out when that commercial came on. I think my grandma would, too."

The ad she is referring to, for the fast-food chain Carl's Jr.'s Spicy BBQ Six Dollar Burger, featured Hilton washing a car seductively in a barely there bathing suit. Kay, the previously mentioned forty-five-year-old nursing student from Missouri, didn't like it. "This commercial is showing disrespect for women. Women are shown as sex objects and not as intelligent human beings. Carl's Jr. has made the decision to market their product to men without concern for the alienation of female customers. They actually don't risk much, because too many young women don't realize the message this sends. Young girls grow up with the idea that it is more important to look good than to become educated, because that is how women gain importance in a man's world."

True, most of the advertisements for fast food, soda, pizza, chips, and beer have a male sensibility, because these are key products that men buy for themselves, without a woman guiding the decision. However, since younger women like Christina, Tesia, and Heidi are less likely to be offended by sexuality and crudeness, these ads are no longer as polarizing as they once were, and they might actually be attracting young women to the brands. I asked Christina if she thought her generation was pushing more boundaries than women of previous generations did. "I don't know," she answered. "I would have said yes before I started working at the beauty shop. But the more I work here, and the more I hear [older] women talk about what they did when they were younger, it sounds just like my girl-friends talking."

I asked 30-plus women if they thought today's teens and twenty-somethings were any more rebellious, crude, and sexualized than previous generations. I got a mixed bag of replies. Colorado college professor Miranda said, "I'm not a big fan of the whole 'the new generation's gone to shit' argument." Miranda told me that she believes that television shows and movies portray young people as more sexualized and rebellious than they actually are. When she evaluates the young people in her classroom, she doesn't see reality in those representations. Thirtysomething Kelly, who is married and lives in Venice, California, believes that the culture has changed, but doesn't believe Generation Y is more affected by it. "The reality TV culture has affected all of us. There are things that would have offended me ten years ago that don't now because I think we've evolved. It's changed all of us. It's not exclusive to Generation Y."

Nicole, a mother of two from Arizona, told me that every generation behaves a bit more recklessly than the previous generation because teens naturally want to be rebellious. She wondered how much further today's teens can push the envelope. "Because so many things have already been done that are rebellious, they just have to go that much further."

"If you look at sitcoms, movies, the way we dress, the language we use—it's become a more informal culture," women's marketing expert Marylou Quinlan said. I asked *Advertising Age* columnist and ad reviewer Bob Garfield if he agreed. "Unequivocally, the society and discourse have coarsened. If you used the word 'suck' when I was in school you would have been probably expelled. Now they don't even care if you spell it right, and there is much more tolerance for vulgarity and violence and pornography. . . . as a result, it has become more difficult for advertising to pack a punch. . . . In a culture where porn stars are celebrities, it's harder and harder to break through the noise, and it puts more pressure on [advertisers] to be obnoxious," he said.

Case in point: A 2007 ad campaign for the menswear company Haggar centered on two blue-collar guys seeking revenge on all of the slackers and Richie Riches who cross them. In one commercial, one of the guys slaps a lump of dog poop into his annoying neighbor's hand. While Haggar is a outfitter for men, its advertising is still probably meant for the eyes of women, since statistics show that women make more than 80 percent of all household purchases. Clothing purchases, even men's clothing, are probably still part of that equation.

Garfield gave the Haggar ads a scathing review in his weekly column. Writing directly to Haggar and the firm who created the ad, Crispin Porter & Bogusky, Garfield asked them, "Have you no sense of boundaries? Have you no sense of decorum? Have you no sense of respect? At long last, have you no sense of shame?"[8] I asked Garfield why he was so tough on the ad. "It's indefensible, because advertising is an uninvited guest where it appears, and it has a responsibility for decorum, and it has no right to barge into your house, showing someone smearing dog shit into someone else's hand."

"But don't some girls [and guys] like the show off?" I asked him. He replied, "Sometimes there is one girl in class who secretly admires the class clown," he answered, "but the minute he wipes shit on another classmate, he is lost to her forever."

Because of decency standards on American television, there are limits on how far advertisers can take jokes and sexual innuendos in their commercial content. The Haggar ad probably went as far as it could go. However, because the web is unregulated, it has become a new home for edgier advertising. The online ads that are sometimes called "viral videos" are designed to be so funny, outrageous, or just plain weird that viewers aren't able to resist emailing the ads to their friends. The file-sharing site YouTube is where many of these ads are discovered. And because YouTube has become such a worldwide sensation, many companies are creating viral ads exclusively for the web, with naughty story lines that would never get past American television censors.

Consider a viral video from Remington, which makes haircare products. The company hired the marketing firms Grey London and the Viral Factory to produce a long-form commercial that was shot to look like a documentary, offering a behind-the-scenes look at a fashion show. As the commercial unfolds, we learn that the fictional designer is not showing any clothing on the runway. Rather, he is a hairstylist who specializes in pubic hair design. (Yes, you read that right.) Then we watch the models walk down the runway nude, modeling only their sculpted, dyed, and permed pubic hair, which they claim to have grown for weeks prior to the runway show. The Viral Factory reported that the ad had gotten nearly two and a half million hits within its first three weeks of being posted to the web.

In terms of decency, Garfield told me he has fewer objections to the content in viral ads, because viewers are more likely to be aware of what is to come. "There is a lot more room for edgy, confrontational, show-offy behavior in the viral form than there is in any kind of broadcast. So that's good news for all the assholes out there," he said.

Those who work in this segment of the advertising world say there is no silver bullet in producing a buzz-worthy viral video. The medium is in a gold rush state, as companies only randomly strike gold. There are few rules for scoring a hit. Kevin Roddy, executive creative director of BBH, told *Fortune* magazine, "I believe if you want to be successful in the world of viral, you need to play by the rules of entertainment, not the rules of selling. A lot of brands might have difficulty with that. But as soon as you [sell], [consumers] say, 'Well, I'm not going to do your [advertising] work for you.'"[9] Perhaps Owen Plotkin, president of a New York–based editing firm that creates television commercials and viral ads, said it best when he told *The New York Times,* "The sophomoric, shock-driven work is going to predominate for a while. . . . That's the easiest way to ensure people pass something along."[10]

Beyond the content, Garfield said viral advertising also involves a different business strategy. It's relatively inexpensive to produce these ads. While it is much more expensive to buy airtime on the television networks and radio, and space in magazines and newspapers, posting videos on the web is free. So advertisers are producing many more online videos and hoping that something will stick.

Will Jeffery, founder of the U.K.-based viral production company Maverick Media, said that there are obvious benefits to going viral, and few risks, since the cost is so low. "It's a much more direct way of speaking to people," Jeffery said. "It costs them much less than booking spots on television. It also allows advertisers who are smaller to come into the space, because they can't afford television. And it's great, because they are getting the consumers to advocate for their content by passing it around."

When viral videos first came out in the late '90s, he said, viewers passed everything they received to their friends, because videos were a novelty at that time. "I don't believe that novelty exists to the same extent," he said, telling me that there are now approximately sixty-thousand clips uploaded daily on YouTube. That means the viral landscape is massively overpopulated, making it difficult for consumers to discover ads, and for ads to stick. Because of this, Maverick Media does not aim for its viral ads to reach millions of men and women of all ages. Rather, it creates viral ads that will reach its clients' target audience. So, while viral advertising is a relatively new form of advertising, Jeffery said, its success hinges on good old-fashioned targeting. A viral ad for, say, a specific brand of lipstick is only meant to appeal to the brand's target consumers, twentysomething women. Maverick staffers are charged with thinking of relevant viral content for the twentysomething female segment. The content must be useful and/or entertaining enough to motivate the consumers to pass it along to their friends. If, let's say, the hypothetical lipstick ad spread to several thousand young women, it would be considered a success. If that ad made a huge splash, reaching millions of women and men, that would be fine too. It would be a happy accident.

Distribution is key. YouTube has a reach as broad as network television's. It reaches the masses, but that isn't narrow enough to assure a company that its brand's target consumers are being reached. So viral firms like Maverick are developing segmented online networks of consumers. Over time, consumers who enjoy Maverick's content send the company their demographic information and email addresses. Maverick also rewards consumers who give the company their information. Jeffery created a website called The Viral Chart to track the most-viewed viral videos and advertisements online. The company's technology is able to sum the number of hits that viral videos are receiving on Google Video, YouTube, and a few other popular video-sharing sites. The Viral Chart then ranks the viral videos according to those that are viewed most. "It's very important to clients to benchmark their results," he said, explaining that each time Maverick creates a viral ad for a company, that client always wants to know how its number of hits compares with others.

Heidi, the aforementioned liberal schoolteacher from Salt Lake City, went online to look at some of the popular ads ranked on The Viral Chart, as well as other ads floating around on YouTube. There she saw Dove's Evolution ad, which has had tremendous success, reaching millions of women via the web. In fast-forward style, it shows how an average-looking woman is transformed into a model with the help of hours of makeup and hairstyling, as well as Photoshop computer technology used to enlarge her eyes, lengthen her neck, and hide flaws.

A viral ad for Norelco talks about all of the places on your body that could use a trim, courtesy of Norelco's new Bodygroom product. Dressed in a white bathrobe and speaking in a full-on announcer voice, the clean-cut man in the ad speaks directly to the camera and unabashedly says, "The Philips Bodygroom has a sleek, ergonomic design for a safe and easy way to trim those scruffy underarm hairs, the untidy curls on and around your [bleep], as well as the hard-to-reach locks on the underside of your [bleep] and [bleep]." As each dirty word is bleeped, an image of a carrot, peach, or a pair of kiwis flashes on the screen next to the man. Though the ad is geared more toward men, Heidi was quite fond of it. She even thought Norelco could have gone further. "I thought it was odd that the Norelco ad was censored. I'm surprised that they just didn't say [the dirty words]. I think I would have enjoyed it more, along with the fruit diagrams," she said. "But if I had been with my ninety-year-old grandmother, even in its censored state, I think she would have been offended." Heidi told me that she thought her older sister and her mom would be fine with the ad, although her mom could go either way: "She is a coin toss on this kind of stuff," she said.

The Bodygroom viral campaign has been very successful, according to Philips Norelco executives. While the company expected to sell four thousand units in the first year, the cheeky campaign led Norelco to sell six thousand units in the first six weeks. Better still, the campaign cost less than $500,000 to produce. Distributing the ad cost next to nothing, thanks to the web.[11] The Norelco ad purposely mocked the outdated sales-pitchy announcer voice common in ads from the past, which would talk about a product's attributes ad nauseum.

When viral ads aren't making fun of this outdated announcer-voice style, they are avoiding it altogether. Heidi noticed that most of the viral ads she viewed didn't mention the name of the product at all. "They try to make it more of a story, rather than 'Here's our product, and here's why you have to have it,'" Heidi said. "As far as entertainment value, I do prefer that, but now I don't remember the product." She told me about seeing an online ad for Burger King that showed a man slither across the floor like a snake and eat another person's Triple Whopper in one enormous bite. "I like the image, and it's really funny, but I wouldn't remember Burger King," she said. "But if you don't have TiVo, you're forced to watch [commercials], and in that case, it's better to have it be entertaining, because at least you aren't changing the channel." Heidi understood the quandary marketers are in, and why they at times choose entertainment content at the expense of name recognition. However, companies have been successful at accomplishing both feats. For example, Geico ran ads where real customers tell positive stories about working with the insurance company, as quirky celebrities join in and embellish the ads in their own hilarious ways.

In one commercial, we see a woman named Denise sitting at her kitchen table, having breakfast with none other than Little Richard, who breaks into the story several times to hoot and holler. In another Geico commercial, a man named Stanley talks about being devastated after wrecking his car, as Charo reenacts the story in classic Charo style. The ads were funny, and, more important, the focus was Geico's customer service. In a Doritos commercial that ran during the 2007 Super Bowl, a checkout girl flirts with a male customer who is buying several bags of Doritos, all in new flavors. The checkout girl is slightly overweight, cute, and charming, but is not the typical sexpot seen in most Super Bowl ads. As she scans each bag of Doritos, she comments on the flavors. She tells him the Nacho Cheese bag is "old school," and the new Habañero chips are "hot!" As she scans the Blazing Buffalo Ranch Doritos, she looks at him seductively and says, "Giddyup." As she scans the Salsa Verde Doritos, she says the word "verde" with a fake accent, rolling the letter "r" in a seductive growl. He likes it and growls back. Audiences liked the comedic timing. All along, the message was still focused on the Doritos. No one could forget the Salsa Verde.

Interestingly, the Doritos ad was not created by an expensive ad firm hired by Doritos. A consumer created it and submitted it to Frito-Lay as part of a company-sponsored contest. Many companies are experimenting with contests, as they are finding that many average Joes are creating ads for their own amusement and running them on You-Tube and other file-sharing sites. It's become so commonplace that the industry has a term for it: "consumer-generated advertising." Wannabe short-film creators are becoming makeshift ad executives, creating their own online versions of commercials they see on television. Other web users are merely using everyday consumer products in amateur videos, which they are posting online.

When browsing YouTube, I found numerous parodies of the Dove Evolution viral ad. One showed a good-looking young man morph into an overweight version of himself by drinking massive amounts of alcohol and eating junk food in fast-forward speed. Another showed a pumpkin endure a series of carvings and Photoshop corrections until it turned into a human face. Other popular clips on YouTube use branded products in their odd and sometimes irreverent videos. For example, after typing "McDonald's" into the search section of YouTube, I found videos created by users that were not ads, but were rather pieces of entertainment for others to enjoy. One video, called "Speed Painting with Ketchup and French Fries," showed a man create a painting in fifty minutes, using only McDonalds fries as his paintbrush and the ketchup as paint. It was viewed more than one million times. Another ad, called "Fast-Food Freestyle," showed a man pulling a prank at his local McDonald's, rapping his order into the drive-through speaker box. It was viewed more than four million times.

In the YouTube universe, these videos have the potential to become overnight hits, garnering millions of views as people around the world download the videos. Companies have long been accustomed to protecting and controlling their brand messages. But videos like these are forcing them to give up some of this control. Marketing veteran Steve Hall said one of the best examples is a series of videos on YouTube that demonstrates the large explosion created by dropping a pack of Mentos into a bottle of Diet Coke. These videos became extremely popular. Hundreds of thousands of people have since viewed Mentos/Diet Coke videos, or created their own videos when experimenting with the ingredients. Hall explained that the Mentos company was smart, immediately embracing the phenomenon. The company created its own Mentos Geyser video contest, which it ran from the Mentos website. The company also spoke favorably about the videos to the press.

Women's marketing expert and author Marylou Quinlan told me that inherent risks come with less traditional content in advertising. "Women don't like to exclude each other, so 'edgy' is sometimes a loner strategy, because it tends to be an I-don't-care-what-everyone-thinks-about-me thing," she said. "I don't think that is very appealing for many women. Because women have the skill of being inclusive. They are the calming person in the office, the glue in the family. It might be funny every once in a while, but when it's hurtful to others, you start to lose women."

Several marketing experts who specialize in the female market brought to my attention a commercial for the Hummer H3. The commercial shows a mom on the playground with her young son, Jake. Another mom is there with her son, who cuts in front of Jake as he approaches the slide. That prompts Jake's mom to say, "I'm sorry, Jake was next." The other mom responds by saying, "Yeah, well, we're next now." In a series of quick cuts, we see Jake and Mom head to the Hummer dealership, where they buy a Hummer H3. Mom straps Jake into his car seat and drives away with a very satisfied look on her face. Then a graphic comes up that reads, "Get your girl on."

"[The creators] probably thought it was really funny," expert Andrea Learned said. "But that humor seems really mean-spirited and probably won't work with women." That was confirmed for me when I went to a few websites, including one called Commercialsihate.com. One person wrote, "So if the other mommies don't like you, get a Hummer, and then your spoiled little spawn will have friends. Grrrr. . . . " Another wrote, "These commercials insult me in so many ways that I can barely explain them all." Hummer received a spattering of other complaints online.

I found that the web is a wasteland of angry blog and message-board postings about advertisements. It makes it difficult to know which of the show-off ads are particularly inflammatory. The most obvious offenders are the ones that are pulled from the television airwaves after receiving broader criticism in the media, and through scores of hand-written complaint letters and phone calls to the company. For example, in early 2007, Washington Mutual ran a commercial that showed supposed bankers contemplating suicide by jumping off of a building. Soon, after receiving complaints from various organizations, including the American Foundation for Suicide Prevention, the bank withdrew the commercial.[12] A 2007

Super Bowl commercial for Snickers showed two male mechanics accidentally kiss, prompting them to gasp in horror and tear hair from their chests to prove their manliness. The candymaker Mars, which owns the Snickers brand, withdrew the commercial the day after the Super Bowl because the company received so many complaints from the public.

Marketing veteran and blogger Holly Buchanan told me that sometimes companies get so caught up in being outlandish that they don't tie the content of their commercial to the product or the brand's overall message. In early 2007, the Canadian branch of the consumer products haircare brand Sunsilk released a viral video on YouTube that was meant to look like a home video of a bride and bridesmaids getting ready before the wedding. The enraged bride has just come back from the hairstylist and tells her bridesmaids that she hates her hair. Over the course of the six-minute video, which is captured by one of the bridesmaids, the bride gets more and more angry, using profanity and finally resorting to cutting off her hair as her bridesmaids watch in horror. In reality, Sunsilk hired actresses to make the video, which was posted online to build buzz for a television commercial Sunsilk later released about "hair wig-outs." Sunsilk products were meant to be the solution to these kinds of embarrassing situations. Because Sunsilk's bridezilla wig-out was produced to look like a real home video, the Sunsilk brand was never mentioned.[13] So, while it was watched more than a million times online and was mentioned on *The Tonight Show with Jay Leno* and *Good Morning America,* the Sunsilk brand wasn't always connected to the publicity. Some news stories were reported about the video. Those stories mainly focused on how YouTube viewers were fooled and didn't realize that the realistic video was created by Sunsilk. A Sunsilk spokesperson, Geoff Craig, told the Canadian news agency CTV News, "We understand very much that women have these moments with their hair, and some of them end up in what we're calling 'wig-outs.'" He added, " . . . It was certainly never our intent to do anything other than provide a dramatization of one of these moments from the get-go."[14]

Other brands have been able to make a statement while connecting their brand and message to the content. Nike aired a commercial with tennis pro Maria Sharapova, set to the song "I Feel Pretty" from *West Side Story*. The commercial shows onlookers singing the song sweetly while a tough-faced Sharapova enters a tennis arena, ignoring them. Sharapova never says a word, but rather lets her game speak for itself when she hits a whopper of a serve, silencing everyone's singing. "The perception is that [because of her beauty] she isn't serious about the game. [Nike] could ignore it or take it head on, and I love that they took it head on," Buchanan said, reiterating what all of the other experts say: Great marketing to women is transparent and authentic. "I think there is this sense of 'Be honest with me; be ethical.' Women are saying, 'Do you walk the walk, talk the talk?'"

But Buchanan added that, in today's marketing world, honesty and edginess only go so far. "I think 27 percent of households are headed up by single mothers. Why are commercials so afraid to show a family without a dad?" she asked, suggesting that most marketers believe that showing a single mom would be bad for their strategies. "It takes guts to go and show something [like this], because when you test these kinds of ads [with focus groups], they tend not to test well. They can be polarizing. Half the group will say, 'Thank you for showing this; this is what my life looks like,' and the other half says, 'Where is the dad?'"

A Ford commercial that broke the mold shows a happy family coming home from an outing together. Mom is driving. The car pulls up to the driveway and Dad gets out, waves happily, and goes into his home. Mom and kids wave goodbye and drive away. We realize that the parents are actually divorced but are friendly toward each another, à la Bruce and Demi. It was a favorite of stay-at-home Virginia mom Jody as she considered getting a divorce from her husband. She told me that the commercial gave her hope that her family could still be considered normal and happy, even if she and her husband could not live under the same roof. This commercial stood out, since most advertising scenarios continue to show a family with both a mother and a father, despite the reality that many children have parents who are divorced. Nontraditional households are now the majority in America. According to U.S. Census figures analyzed by *The New York Times* in 2005, there was a higher percentage of unmarried couples than married couples living in U.S. households.[15]

Most of the women I spoke to agreed that they would like to see fewer traditional families in advertising. Fortysomething Melanie, who lives near Chattanooga, Tennessee, said, "Representations of nontraditional families don't bother me. I know people in real life who are nontraditional, so it seems normal." Twentysomething Maria, from Miami, said, "I would definitely prefer to see [fewer] traditional families portrayed in ads. I think that advertising should reflect and imitate life; it's a healthy extension of the medium and it allows everybody, regardless of their situation, to feel connected. Advertising is its own language, and if it doesn't correctly reflect the present and all the wonderful diversity in the world, then it fails to hit the mark. Also, and this may sound a little extreme, we should be mindful of the way future generations look back historically on the advertising of our generation. What will they see? Will it accurately portray our reality, or [will it be] a skewed version of who we really are?"

Fifty-four-year-old Barbara, from Pittsburgh, said she too would like to see nontraditional families in ads, even though she has mostly traditional values. Ads that show single parents and grandparents raising children are part of life, she told me. "And it's important to reinforce that that's okay." Barbara is single and has never married or had children. But throughout her life, Barbara has seen women her age portrayed in ads solely as mothers and wives. Some ads show grown children coming home to their parents' house for family gatherings. This kind of traditional content in ads has never been particularly relevant to Barbara. She would be happily shocked to someday see a nontraditional approach—an ad that shows an extended family coming to an aunt's home for a family dinner or celebration. It would reflect her reality.

Despite how far America has come in celebrating diversity and today's reality, companies are still reluctant to show nontraditional families and mixed-race couples in their advertisements, even as census figures show that these groups exist and are growing tremendously. The U.S. Census Bureau has measured the number of children living in mixed-race families since 1970 and has found that the number has doubled each decade, growing from 460,000 in 1970 to nearly three million in 2000.[16] The census also revealed that from 1970 to 2000, the number of single mothers increased from three million to ten million. This census report also found that one-third of lesbian households and one-fifth of gay households include children. However, mixed-race people and nontraditional families are rarely portrayed in advertising.

Ads that do show nontraditional families and ethnic diversity are viewed as novelties, to the point of garnering media coverage. For example, in 2002 a reporter wrote about a string of Kmart commercials that featured people of many different races. One of the ads included the company's first portrayal of a mixed-race family: an Asian mother, a European American father, and their daughter.[17] Another story covered a series of Verizon commercials that showed a European American dad and a Latina mom.[18] The aforementioned Ford "divorce commercial" was covered by *The New York Times*. The article also described a commercial for the drug Nexium, in which a single dad prepares dinner for his children. The *Times* pointed out that in the past, divorced dads were depicted as deadbeats in ads, but that the Ford and Nexium ads represented an image overhaul.

Again, these examples are the exceptions in the world of advertising. More often, companies stray from showing these real-life situations because they are fearful that their advertising will alienate their customers, cause a media firestorm, or elicit a boycott by conservative groups. Marketers look to surveys to gauge how their consumers will respond to an ad with a nontraditional message; however, various surveys produce conflicting results.

For example, one study has found that the majority of Americans would not support boycotts started by conservative groups that object to gay-friendly advertising. However, other studies show that the majority of Americans are concerned about nontraditional families. For example, a 2006 Harris Poll commissioned by *Redbook* magazine asked participants if there was more than one way to define the term "family." Seventy-two percent answered yes. In response to a different question, 70 percent said families have changed for the worse since a generation ago. Fifty-three percent said they believed same-sex couples have a negative impact on American family life, and 88 percent said divorce has a negative impact on the family structure.[19] Those stats certainly don't help to convince a company to run a commercial that shows a positive portrayal of a divorced or same-sex family.

Companies are also reticent to advertise on controversial television shows and countercultural mediums. For example, in 2004, Lowe's and Tyson withheld their ads from *Desperate Housewives* during the show's first season because they believed it was too racy. In 2005, the American

Family Association (AFA) pressured the Ford Motor Company to stop advertising in gay media, and boycotted the company. Ford initially said it would stop advertising its Jaguar and Land Rover lines in gay media, but reversed its decision and said it would advertise all of its automobile lines in gay media.[20]

In a different case, a couple of broadcast networks declined to run a 2007 commercial for Trojan condoms. The ad showed men depicted as pigs at a bar, trying to pick up women. When one of the pigs went to the bathroom and bought a condom from a vending machine, he magically turned into a good-looking guy. The ads conveyed that by being prepared with a condom, men evolve from animals to humans, especially in the eyes of the opposite sex. Fox and CBS would not run the ads on their networks, even late at night. CBS told Trojan it didn't find the ad to be appropriate. Fox told Trojan, "Contraceptive advertising must stress health-related uses, rather than the prevention of pregnancy." The 2001 Kaiser Family Foundation report on condom advertising found that some networks allow condom ads that focus on disease prevention, and reject ads about pregnancy prevention, because they could be considered controversial for religious and moral reasons."[21] This seemed to be the case, since Fox and CBS allowed previous Trojan ads that advised condom use to prevent sexually transmitted diseases. Carol Carrozza, the vice president of marketing for the company that makes LifeStyles condoms, told *The New York Times,* "We always find it funny that you can use sex to sell jewelry and cars, but you can't use sex to sell condoms."

At least part of the reason networks are hesitant to air condom ads is to prevent boycotts from conservative groups such as the AFA and Focus on the Family. It is difficult to know whether boycotts by these groups significantly affect a company's bottom line. The AFA boycotted Disney for nine years after the corporation decided to provide same-sex benefits for its workers; however, Disney sales did not slump. In other cases, the AFA has successfully steered companies to change their advertising. In 2006, the CEO of T-Mobile agreed to pull its advertising from the FX cable network following a slew of complaint emails from the AFA.[22] The conservative group objected to two of the network's edgier programs, *Rescue Me* and *It's Always Sunny in Philadelphia,* which include adult themes and language. The AFA appeared to have a hand in big-box retailer Target's decision to use the word "Christmas" in its advertising, rather than the broader word "holiday."[23] In addition, I came across numerous news stories from the past few years that noted how executives from various large corporations met with AFA representatives to reach an agreement in order to prevent a boycott by the group's two million members.

Changes in the way corporations hire and fire their advertising firms are also tightening the reins on ad creators who want to reflect a more liberal or realistic point of view. Marketing consultant Kimberly McCall told me that if companies aren't seeing results with their firm of the moment, they move on quickly. She called it "agency jumping," and said, these days, there are few second chances. "Companies are looking for the new hot agency. They want to see something different. I've seen it across the board, from the hundred-person company to the giants. . . . There is just that client ADD. They want something hipper, cooler, faster, better. And the churn is there, no matter what the agency."

I understood what McCall was referring to, having kept up with *Advertising Age,* the primary trade magazine for the marketing industry. Once or twice a week, I would run across a story about a major company dropping its ad firm or hiring a new one. It was clear to me that there was tension between ad firms and their corporate clients. In 2007, a Forrester Research survey reported that only 21 percent of companies would recommend their advertising agency to others. However, many of the companies had no concrete way to know whether their ad firm was failing them. The report found that 76 percent of the companies surveyed had no way to determine whether they were getting a good return on their dollar. Sixty-nine percent said that return on investment (also known in the industry as ROI) is too difficult to measure.

"There's always an undercurrent of discontent with agencies," Peter Kim, a senior analyst at Forrester, said in a February 2007 *Advertising Age* story. "What surprised me is that three-quarters [of firms surveyed] do not measure agency ROI. They're dissatisfied, yet on what basis? It's not because the agency didn't help them drive sales or meet some other business outcome. It's a vague disenchantment or disappointment; it's a feeling that there isn't data to back up."[24]

I wanted to know more about why companies so often switch ad firms. I wrote to advertising veteran Steve Hall, looking for an answer. He did not mince words in his email back to me. "The answer is very simple: ego," he wrote. "A new marketing director joins a brand and they want to make their mark. Easiest way? Fire the old agency because, of course, it must have sucked." Hall explained that the advertising business has become very fickle, and marketing leaders at companies choose more often to completely change the company's ad strategy than to rejuvenate what is currently in place. But this strategy can be problematic, since consumers are never given enough time to understand the new brand before it changes again.

Hall continued, "That's a big problem in the industry. No one believes in the power of longevity any longer, and that it takes years, even decades, to solidify a strong and well-understood brand message among those people who are the company's customers. When I was working in agencies and we heard a new marketing director had been hired at one of our clients, I'd just throw in the towel, knowing the inevitable would happen. It always did. It's dumb. It's childish. Welcome to the elementary playground of the advertising industry."

So, to save their necks, ad executives are only going edgy and authentic to a point, shocking audiences with safer sophomoric comedy instead of glaring reality. However, by not showing accurate portrayals of family life today, advertisers are shaping how Americans—especially young, impressionable Americans—determine what is normal. Divorce may not be ideal, but the many children of divorced parents deserve to see their lives normalized by a positive ad that shows a divorced family. The Ford commercial that showed the divorced family was part of a 2006 ad campaign that ad firm JWT created and called Bold Moves; it didn't lead to better sales. Ford's domestic sales declined by 8 percent,[25] although that decline is probably due to more than the ads in the Bold Moves campaign.

Hats off to Ford for having the courage to run an ad with such a progressive point of view. And by the way, JWT still creates ads for Ford.

CHAPTER 6

The Dreamboat

The Dreamboat always has a trophy girl on his arm. In high school, he dated the cheerleader because she made him a hot commodity. As an adult, he proudly displays his Stepford wife.

Companies are no different. They've long paid models, Hollywood actresses, and ingenues to star in their advertisements. Their hope is that women everywhere will want to buy their products, because if it's good enough for the unattainably perfect girl, it's good enough for the rest of us. Naturally, we will aspire to achieve her perfection, hoping that the product will transform us.

This "perfection message" has been used since the advent of advertising. Pamela Laird, a history professor and author of the book *Advertising Progress,* told me that advertising has existed since merchants have had the need to communicate. In ancient Greece, street criers would stand in the village markets and walk through the streets, telling women that their products would make women beautiful. Laird mentioned a street crier song from that time that translates as: "For eyes that are shining/for cheeks like the dawn/for beauty that lasts after girlhood is gone/for prices in reason/the woman who knows/will buy her cosmetics of Aesclyptoe." Perhaps Aesclyptoe was the Maybelline of his day.

Street crying was a common advertising technique for many centuries. When markets grew in size and newspapers became less expensive to mass-produce (in the 1820s), they replaced street crying in the United States. And again, messages of perfection appeared in print advertising throughout the nineteenth century. While many of today's ads promise that a product will make a person more attractive or successful, transformation was never part of the equation in the nineteenth century, except for ads for medicine. Most other ads implied that a purchase was a reflection of a person's character, telling consumers that if they bought the product advertised, it meant that they were already good, successful, attractive people. This message was shaped by the literature and lore of the time, which showed physically ugly characters as the villains and good-looking characters as the heroes, princesses, or protagonists. Therefore, print ads often showed a comparison between a good-looking, fair-skinned person using the advertised brand and an ugly, unhappy, disorganized person using another brand.

Laird gave me an example as she looked at a print ad from that time: "What you have, for example, is an ad for a soap product, and it shows Mrs. Fogy, who is obviously a shrew and unkempt and her baby is crying, whereas Mrs. Enterprise is lovely, and her wash is already done, and she uses the soap that is being advertised." Good mothers in ads were portrayed as nurturing, relaxed, and beautiful, and they were rarely shown working around the house. Ads that did show a mother working implied that her work was pleasant and easy, stressing that the product made her housework easier so that she could be relaxed, kind, and loving to her family. "The problem with this is that it portrayed the ideal woman as a woman who is not laboring hard, which was not realistic for working-class women and middle-class women," Laird said.

These portrayals laid the roots of perfection in advertising, which continued into the twentieth century. Ads from the early twentieth century seemed to claim that a proper woman's housework was easy because her husband was a good provider and gave her the newest products on the market. This made her housework very simple, affording her the time to keep herself looking beautiful, nurturing the children, and being happy. The ads told women that they had no reason to be grouchy, sweaty, or frustrated. This ideal continued throughout much of the twentieth century, and this was reinforced by television shows in the '50s and '60s, such as *Ozzie and Harriet, Leave It to Beaver,* and *The Donna Reed Show.* "Advertising said that happiness was in a bottle of floor wax," women's marketing consultant and author Michele Miller told me. "But when you looked at candid photos of real women in the '50s, you saw women scrubbing the sink with a crying baby on one arm."

"The image of the good mother—the knowing mother, the perfect mother—has been a successful technique for a century now," said women's studies professor Jennifer Scanlon, who has studied images of women in advertising throughout history. She explained that the elements of perfection have changed over time. "Perhaps it was, [at] first, the mother who purchased national brands because they were superior to locally produced, potentially harmful food products. Then it was the mother who kept germs away from her innocent children. Then it was the mother who recognized that adolescents had their own needs, and would allow her little consumers to buy things for themselves."

In later decades of the twentieth century, the good mother was shown as the woman who could juggle a career and take care of the home and children. This image was more prevalent in the 1970s and '80s, as the feminist movement began to impact mass media. Television portrayed independent working women on shows such as *The Mary Tyler Moore Show, Murder She Wrote,* and *Murphy Brown.* Advertising followed the mass media of the time. Ad firms began to value women not only because women were earning their own money, but also because women began taking careers in advertising firms, and those rare women planted seeds of change from within. Female-focused ads from this era included Revlon's perfume ad that proclaimed, "I can bring home the bacon, fry it up in a pan," and Secret's deodorant ads, which bore the slogan "Strong enough for a man, but made for a woman." Female characters in ads were no longer chained to the stove, but they still projected an image of perfection. They were just juggling more duties.

In the '70s and '80s, Laird said, advertisers began to favor younger models, so consumers saw fewer thirty- and fortysomethings as attractive figures in advertising. The prevalence of 18- to 25-year-old models per-petuated and escalated the unattainably perfect message. In the '80s and '90s, supermodels graced the covers of magazines and were prominent in cosmetic ads. Celebrities became an even more prominent part of popular culture, with the growth of tabloid magazines and tabloid-style entertain-ment programs. Women longed to look like the models and celebrities they so often saw in media. Advancements in cosmetic surgery, tanning beds, teeth whitening, and hair extensions during the '80s and '90s made beauty even more unattainable. Advertising, as it always has, followed popular culture.

Advertising Age ad reviewer and columnist Bob Garfield was quite blunt about what is driving the glut of gorgeous, computer-enhanced models in advertising. "Unfortunately, appeals to vanity are the single most successful marketing technique ever conceived," he said. Garfield told me that, like it or not, there are certain tried-and-true techniques that work with women. One is to tell them they will look younger if they use a product, and to show a physically perfect woman in the ad.

Women could be particularly vulnerable to these messages because of how their brains process information, said Michele Miller, who authored *The Natural Advantages of Women,* a book about the female brain. Researchers have long known that women have more brain neurons that connect the left and right sides, making women better at visualization and reading between the lines. More recent research, from the Indiana University School of Medicine, found that while both men and women listen with the left side of the brain, which is associated with speech and listening, women also use the right side of the brain, which is associated with nonlanguage auditory functions.[1] Miller explained it this way on her marketing blog: "[The left] is the side that is concerned with what was just said. The right hemisphere, however, is concerned with how it feels." When I spoke to Miller, she elaborated, telling me that this left and right-brain connection means that women are impacted by advertising because they read into the messaging more deeply and are thinking more emotionally about the message. "So when [women] see an ad that says, *You must be perfect,* whether it's 'Happiness is weighing ninety-eight pounds' or '[Happiness is] owning a pair of Manolos,' women tend to feel that they are supposed to do that."

But it now appears that marketers have gone too far with their messages of perfection. Scanlon explained that women today want to see more authentic representations, " . . . be it women with curves, more women of color, [or] more women of varied ages." When I spoke to women about advertising, their first complaint was about the unattainable images of beauty. That complaint transcended age, size, hair color, race, or hometown. It was this type of outcry that inspired Dove to create the Campaign for Real Beauty, which celebrated women of all shapes and sizes.

Dove's plan to redefine beauty, and dethrone Miss Perfect in the process, began in 2003, when executives came up with a hypothesis. They believed that the definition of beauty was becoming more and more narrow, and that that was a problem for women of all ages. Dove, which is owned by the large consumer-products company Unilever, decided to do its own research to confirm the executives' assumption. The company hired research firm Strategy 360 to conduct "The Real Truth About Beauty"—a study Dove calls one of the largest, most comprehensive studies of women's attitudes about beauty. Women around the world were asked their opinions about beauty. The survey results set the course for Dove's marketing campaign. More than 80 percent of American women surveyed said the media and the advertising industry set an unrealistic standard of beauty that most women can never achieve. Only 2 percent of women considered themselves beautiful.

"When you hear stuff like that, you want to take action," Kathy O'Brien, Dove's marketing director, told me. Dove partnered with Ogilvy, its longtime ad agency, to develop the Campaign for Real Beauty. (Ogilvy is a legendary communications firm, not to be mistaken for the Ogilvie home perm products.) The campaign's framework consisted of three parts: listening to women, sparking a debate, and walking the talk, which was done through ads and the launch of Dove's Self-Esteem Fund. Together, Dove and Ogilvy set out to find everyday women of different sizes, ages, and ethnicities to star in their advertising campaign. In 2004, Dove's dialogue-inducing billboard ads were revealed to the public, showing the women standing in white cotton underwear and bras. None of the women looked like models. All of them wore between a size 6 and size 10.

O'Brien told me that the ultimate goal of the campaign was to make women and girls feel beautiful, though she also admitted, "We're in the business of selling." I asked her what the executives at Dove originally thought of the idea—women in their underwear, cellulite, fat rolls, and all. She, being a corporate voice for the company, wouldn't divulge whether "the suits" at Dove were at all apprehensive. She said, "Once you have all the pieces in place, you've spoken to women, you understand how they are feeling, and you get a fact like only 2 percent of women around the world described themselves as beautiful—when you walk people through the process, it's not very shocking or scary." She did say that most people at Dove thought they were on the verge of something phenomenal as they prepared to launch the campaign. Since its debut, the Campaign for Real Beauty has generated considerable buzz in the mass media, and has sparked discourse about how beauty is defined and how advertising should improve. The campaign has become more than just a series of ads. It's become part of popular culture.

O'Brien didn't think the Campaign for Real Beauty could have existed with such gusto ten or twenty years ago, since images of beauty back in the '80s weren't as blatantly unattainable. Over the past five to ten years, she said, beauty images have become increasingly unachievable, due to computerized photo retouching, which has triggered more angst in women. That angst has made everyday women more enthusiastic about the Campaign for Real Beauty and the dethroning of Miss Perfect.

To engage women of all ages in a dialogue about beauty, self-esteem, perfection, and advertising, Dove created a website called Campaignforrealbeauty.com. On it, one woman wrote, "The advertising industry is perpetuating the image that if you are over a size 0, you're not beautiful. The media only showcases women who look like they haven't eaten in decades. I'm sick of it! Beauty comes in all shapes, colors, and sizes. It's time for the industry to stop feeding us falsehoods and start dealing with reality!" Another wrote, "My biggest pet peeve is the NutriSystem commercial where the woman proudly announces to all, 'I went from a size 4 to a size 2.' She needs a swift kick in the reality butt if you ask me." Another woman wrote, "Perfection is not only about physical beauty, it's also about acceptance. Is acceptance more valuable [to a woman] if felt [from] thousands of people by showing off [her] body in a magazine? Or is acceptance more rewarding when a husband hugs his wife and makes her feel beautiful, inside and out?"

Men have also contributed to the Dove dialogue. On Dove's website, one man wrote, "In the end, all of the pressure and the fake images that [are] presented to us make us less self-confident about the way we look. Guys as well are pressured to have a six-pack and look perfect, and maybe they talk to hot girls because it is a way for them to boost up their own self-esteem (like, 'Look at me. I can get with a hot chick'). The guys that are really worth it will talk to you for who you are."

Along with its attention-getting billboards, the Dove campaign included a collection of television commercials that kept the reality vibe alive, complete with nonmodels and a production style that looked like it could be from a reality show or news interview. One group of commercials for Dove's Energy Glow products featured real men in their average-looking living rooms, looking directly into the camera and describing their wives. In one, a smiling man named Michael tells the camera, "She's the woman I love to see in front of me. It's everything about her. Her body looks so good to me. Her skin makes me weak in the knees. It's the magic that's there. And even to this day, I'm still trying to figure it out." The ad concludes by devoting a few seconds to showing his wife, Nadine. It is obvious that Nadine isn't a model, but is rather a slightly better-than-average-looking woman in flattering clothing, under gorgeous lighting, looking happy and confident. Anyone can see that Nadine is beautiful, especially after hearing her husband explain it so sincerely.

"The Dove ads, and the discussion they have generated, show two things. First, that women are tired of the messages of perfection and realize that the price is too high for attempting to reach it," Scanlon said. "Second, though, I believe the Dove ads show that American consumers still want it all. They want to see real bodies, but they wouldn't be happy if that were all they got. They still want to indulge in the fantasy. I wouldn't say it's a backlash against women. I'd say women have always wanted some of both. Until more and more women were employed in advertising, they were more likely to get more of the fantasy and less of the reality than they are now."

Michele Miller agreed, saying, "I believe in equal rights and not waving the feminism flag. . . . But quite realistically, if you look at the ad agencies, there are not a lot of women doing the decision making, whatever that power of authority is. The throne is held by very few women."

The advertising industry has been known as a boys' club, but women are making headway, albeit slowly. Statistics from the Equal Employment Opportunity Commission (EEOC) found that in 2003, women far outnumbered men in advertising agencies, accounting for 65.8 percent of the workforce. However, women's status in advertising wanes with rank.[2] The survey found that women hold 76.7 percent of all clerical positions in the industry and 58.2 percent of all professional positions, which the EEOC defined as jobs that require a college degree. In middle- to upper-management positions, women represent 47 percent of the jobs. The creative side of the business, which is where the content of ads is brainstormed and decided, is still regarded as very male-dominated. *The New York Times* reported that among the top thirty-three advertising agencies, as ranked by the trade publication *Adweek,* only four agencies have flagship offices with female creative directors.[3] According to a 2005 study by the American Association of Advertising Agencies (AAAA), 265 women held senior managerial positions at the more than 400 agencies (in more than 1,200 offices) that belong to the association. That represents significant growth compared with 1994, when the AAAA conducted the survey for the first time and found that only seventy-three women held senior positions.[4]

The 2005 *Adweek* study revealed that only a handful of female creative directors were working in top management at the thirty-three nationally ranked agencies. When *Adweek* reporter Eleftheria Parpis asked industry professionals why the number was so low and whether gender matters on the creative side, she found that some executives did not want to speak openly about the issue. Others seemed to tiptoe around the issue, as if to make sure they did not appear sexist. Many in the industry told Parpis that "the male-dominated creative departments and the larger agency environments themselves are male bastions; therefore, the women that best succeed in advertising . . . are those who can best operate like a man."[5]

Some of the most outspoken sources in Parpis's story were female creative directors. Susan Hoffman, creative director of Wieden + Kennedy, in Portland, Oregon, said, "You need to be a little tougher in this business. . . . If you are a girlie-girl, this isn't the business for you."[6] Creative director and author Sally Hogshead told Parpis that women naturally try to seek agreement, which doesn't always fare well in the creative process, whereas a man's natural strengths come in confidence and voice, which are embraced in the ad workplace. She said, "It's much more uncomfortable for us as women to embrace the friction that goes with defending your ideas, coming back again and again, succeeding in a very high-pressure environment, within the agency, within the client relationship, and within the creative process as well."[7] Nina DiSesa, former chief creative officer at the firm McCann Erickson, told Parpis that the lack of women in creative director positions is also due to the personal choices women must make. She said, "If you are a really good creative director, you can take the agency to the moon. But in order to do that job well, you have to be available all the time. You can't call it in. If you have a child in a school play, how do you make those decisions?"[8]

This is clearly one reason why there are too few female creative directors in the advertising workplace. However, until ad firms redefine the work constraints associated with the position of creative director, this is not going to change. As a result, a disproportionate number of men will continue to hold the key creative leadership positions in the advertising world.

I spoke to women of all ages about the Dove ads, as well as the unrealistic images of women in advertising, which folks in the ad world call "aspirational" messages. I presumed that all of the women interviewed would say that they disliked aspirational ads. While the vast majority of women gave that response, I was surprised to discover that a few women appreciate an aspirational message, because the ads motivate them in a variety of ways, such as getting into even better shape or being more fearless and proactive. The women who said this were all relatively young, in their twenties or thirties, and they all considered themselves to be quite confident, successful, and/or attractive. Certainly, they were the minority. Of the remainder of the women, those most concerned about aspirational ads were women over fifty.

Fifty-five-year-old Canadian business owner Patricia was one of those women. She told me that ads featuring skinny models and young, dewy skin don't make her feel bad about herself, though she believes that ads flaunting Miss Perfect hurt women on the whole, especially younger women and girls.

Women's marketing expert, consultant, and author Mary Brown said Baby Boomer–aged women like Patricia are receptive to ads that buck perfection and unattainable beauty. "There is a shift that goes on when you hit a certain age. It's 'You know what, I don't need to necessarily be proving myself anymore.' There is a wisdom. Things that are speaking to where she is internally are going to hit a chord with her. All other ads go to the wayside and are ignored or unnoticed."

When I asked Patricia how advertising images of physical perfection affect her today, she said, "I don't want to sound cynical, but I think some of the cosmetics companies, they are moving on to the women over fifty who are buying this stuff, and they are appealing to our vanity in a different way. It's a false sense of having them on our side and empathizing with us, and really, they just want our dollars."

Patricia told me about a L'Oréal commercial featuring Diane Keaton, which, she says, looks to have a soft lens focus and lighting, making Keaton appear more youthful than she actually is. "It's obviously doctored. It's not Diane Keaton raw. It's still made-up beauty. I'm very skeptical now. I still buy the products, based on my trial and if the products feel good to me, but I'm not expecting miracles." While Patricia didn't like the L'Oréal commercial, the company has been praised by critics and Boomer marketing consultants for breaking age barriers by featuring Keaton and Jane Fonda. Patricia also doesn't appreciate L'Oréal's slogan: "Because you're worth it." "It's all about our physical gorgeousness, not about our well-being overall. It's not about self-care. It's about making yourself presentable to other people so that you look perfect. We hang our identities on that. I found how it affected me. I developed very high standards for myself and [I] can drive myself nuts."

Beyond beauty, women have also been fed a daily diet of ads that portray women as the ideal mothers, career women, and wives: Some are seen as jovial married women who delight in their husband's idiocy and enjoy bringing beer and snacks to him on the sofa. Others are seen as cool, fun moms who bring cupcakes to their children's classrooms. Others are shown serving a four-course dinner within minutes of getting home from work.

Patricia is a proud feminist and remembers ads like this affecting her when she was working in the business world in the '70s and '80s. "If we were married, advertising was about being perfect for our husbands and looking after our children. If we wanted to have equality in the early '70s, through the second wave, we had to keep our attractiveness. If we didn't, there was nasty name calling and nasty labels. So we still had to keep ourselves very attractive, factor in our husband's needs—both emotional and sexual—and we paid the price, not only with our own personal image, but also, it worked against our health, because we were so tired and rundown trying to please the images of what we were supposed to be. It made women compare themselves against other women and encouraged competition," she said.

Patricia said that perfectionism was an unfortunate by-product of the feminist movement, though the women leading the movement didn't intend for this perfectionism to exist. The "Have it all" women shown in ads back then were not realistic and gave her unattainable expectations. "I think we were sold a bill of goods," she said. "We were told that we could have the family at home, and a career, and keep a husband satisfied. And there was fallout—to marriages and children and the woman herself. And so there was a lot of guilt. There were consequences. So I'm very sensitive about ads today that show us that we can have everything: beauty, money, health. There are consequences if you're always driving for that."

Now Patricia prefers ads that show aging with grace and ease, while also being realistic. She especially hates ads that show retirement as "being on the beach and the woman is still in her bikini," adding, "I gauge my faith in the product based on how realistic [the company is] about my age . . . . If an ad shows me that I'm supposed to be a superwoman at fifty-five or sixty, I just don't want to buy that. That's what I mean about being more aware of who I am and when I'm being sold a bill of goods."

Nicole, a corporate executive and mother of two children under the age of five, told me that she would like to see portrayals of working women who are balancing it all. Nicole believes this can be done in a way that doesn't make women feel inadequate, but rather inspires women like her who are climbing the corporate ladder. "From the ads I see, most women are stay-at-home moms. And granted, they are active and they are running around all day, but I don't feel like there are any corporate moms showing how they juggle it all," she said. "I'm just not wanting to see the stereotypical mom who is worried about cleaning her house. There is more to life than that." The ads Nicole sees that feature women in a business environment don't represent her. "Even though you see the trendy girl getting ready for work, you don't see her in the CEO role. She's not walking in and being the boss." Nicole hasn't given up on the "Have it all" mantra of the past. "There are days when I feel like, *Dammit, yes, we should have it all. There is no reason why we can't.*"

Other women told me that "Have it all" images of advertising seep into their consciousness, causing them to question whether they are living up to society's expectations. Are they successful enough at work? Are they pretty enough? Slim enough? Are they organized enough to juggle all of their responsibilities? Is their home clean enough? Are their families as happy and cooperative as the ones shown in commercials? Thirty-four-year-old Clarissa, from Santa Monica, California, admitted that over the course of her life, she has made numerous life choices based on her need to look perfect to others. After her family emigrated from Korea, her parents focused on her education, and Clarissa knew that they expected her to earn a post-graduate degree at a prestigious university. "So I went to college, majored in psychology, and dabbled in psychobiology, even though I was horrible in science," she said with a laugh. "I think it was the prestige factor." After college, Clarissa earned a master's degree and enrolled in law school, in part to meet the perfect man. "I thought it would be a really great way to meet someone. It sounds really sad and shallow, but it is really true. I wanted to get married to another Asian American professional. And I had this list of what I wanted in a man." Clarissa did marry an Asian man, who fit the list perfectly, but she divorced him because she realized she wasn't happy. She moved out of his large home and into a one-bedroom apartment. She's given up on the image of perfection and has never been happier.

Thirty-one-year-old Miranda, from Colorado, told me she often feels inadequate because of the images she sees in advertising. "I definitely feel bad after seeing ads. I always feel fat," she said. "I think, *Wow, there are women with beautiful skin, and they are so well put-together in terms of their weight and proportion.*" The exception is Nike ads. Miranda finds them inspiring, even though they also show beautiful, thin women. "Their ads are about challenging my body and my mind in some way. And I don't feel inadequate. I feel like it's attainable. Weighing eighty-five pounds is not attainable. And I will never have big breasts. When I see a Nike ad, I feel a little more empowered. I can be strong to meet those physical goals. I like the idea of saying to women that feeling powerful is more important than being a stick figure. That is what is beautiful. When I buy a sports bra, I'm going to pick Nike, because I value the way they represent me."

Internationally recognized consumer advocate and author Jean Kilbourne has spent more than thirty years studying advertising's effects on women and educating consumers. She told me that the most harmful messages in advertising include the objectification of women, the emphasis on the ideal of beauty, the obsession with thinness, and the relentless sexualization of women and girls. However, most consumers don't think these messages have any impact on them. "Advertising remains so powerful because everyone thinks they are too smart for it," Kilbourne said. "They think that they are above it. I often hear, 'Oh, I just tune ads out.' But while people truly believe that, the ad is doing its work."

In her book *Can't Buy My Love,* Kilbourne offers hundreds of examples of ads that have appeared in the media over the past fifty years, and she argues that many advertisements come with destructive side effects, hurting the self-image of men and women and exacerbating eating disorders and addiction in our country.[9] Statistics about how advertising has hurt consumers is largely unavailable. Kilbourne explained that research is scarce because there are no control groups out there. In other words, advertising is so widespread that there are very few people or groups who haven't been exposed to it. Therefore, there is no scientific way to compare people who have been exposed to advertising with those who haven't.

Kilbourne believes we are currently living in an era where advertising messages are at their most harmful levels. "Everything I've been saying for over thirty years is true and, in many ways, worse than ever," she said. This is in part because consumers are exposed to more ads today. Some experts estimate that we see and hear five thousand advertising messages each day, everything from product packaging to signs, from logos to actual advertisements.

Technology also plays a part. As Dove's Evolution ad shows, advertisers can use photo-altering software to change the physical features of models, making them look even more perfect than they already are. This is much more sophisticated than airbrushing out wrinkles. Today's photo altering can change a person's skin tone, hair length, body shape, and eye size. "They couldn't do that thirty years ago, but they can do it now, and so the ideal is less attainable than ever before," Kilbourne told me.

One of the few positive changes in advertising is that the "demented housewife" stereotype doesn't exist anymore, she said, recalling commercials from the 1950s through the '70s that portrayed women obsessed with clean floors and "ring around the collar." But aside from that, the ideal image of beauty—what Kilbourne calls "the tyranny of the aesthetic ideal"—is worse now than ever before.

As for the have-it-all woman from the '70s—the one who brought home the bacon and fried it up in the pan—Kilbourne said, "The superwoman image was harmful because it made it seem as if it should be easy to do it all if you used the right products. If you bought Hamburger Helper, you could work sixty-hour weeks and take care of your children. It created a myth of what is possible." Her statement reiterates what Jennifer Scanlon told me about the ads from the early twentieth century that used that same message: A product could make an ungodly amount of work suddenly simple. And if it was still hard work, there must be something wrong with you.

"Women are often made to feel it is all our fault if we aren't able to do everything perfectly: look beautiful, be very thin, bring in a lot of money, bake cookies from scratch, and raise the children," Kilbourne said. "And advertising promotes this illusion because it's in their [own] best interest to do so."

When I asked most marketing professionals and other experts if they thought companies would emulate Dove's approach, they all told me that it would depend on the bottom line, because while Dove might have good intentions, few advertising firms and companies care more about self-esteem than about sales. In an interview with me, *Advertising Age* columnist Bob Garfield summed it up, saying, "Speaking to women like they are human beings is a nascent trend; once it's ascertained that Dove is increasing sales, you will see copycatting." Jean Kilbourne said, "It depends on how much soap the ads sell. Madison Avenue is not concerned with social change. They are concerned with profit."

Dove's approach goes against conventional marketing wisdom, which says that supportive messages work against the bottom line. According to Kilbourne, "Advertising depends on making us feel anxious and insecure. People who feel good about themselves are less likely to need to buy a lot of stuff." It is for this reason that Scanlon believes many advertisers are unsettled by the enthusiasm for Dove. "It goes against their gut approach of aspirational advertising. [Advertisers] have a lot to fear if we become too happy with who we are. How else will they peddle their wares?" she said. Even consumers were posing this question. New Yorker Camille told me that after Dove ran its billboards on the New York City subways, passersby scribbled comments on top of the ads, many of which challenged Dove. One said something like, "If this is real beauty, then why do they need your product?" Clearly, advertisers are in a damned-if-you-do, damned-if-you-don't situation. If they give women the supportive, attainable images they are asking for, they will not only invite skeptics, but they will also risk their sales.

On the website Soflow.com—a networking website that has since closed down—a group of marketing professionals, both men and women, interacted with one another about issues in their industry, sharing opinions about today's campaigns, posting available jobs, and promoting upcoming seminars. I joined the discussion group so I could occasionally ask marketing-related questions. The question I asked that produced the most responses was about perfection. I asked the online marketing community whether perfection is still an effective marketing technique, or whether today's women are rejecting perfection to the point that it doesn't work anymore.

In just a couple of days, the question elicited more than twenty highly charged comments, and contributors were split on the topic. Kristi Erban, who works for a direct response agency, wrote, "As a female, while I do like the Dove campaign utilizing 'real women,' I still tend to be drawn more towards the ads that feature traditional models. While I am intelligent enough to realize that this level of perfection is not attainable by simply purchasing the featured product, I am also conditioned to see these types of models in ads. I do feel that the advent of 'reality TV' is turning the tide for advertising. Ten years ago our only exposure to entertainment was seeing the 'beautiful people' onscreen. Now our new superstars can be the average Joe, which is redefining our perspective on what popular culture defines as 'famous.'"

Richard Laurence Baron, an advertising copywriter, wrote, "People say one thing and do another. Example: the long-running 'ring around the collar' advertising campaign for Wisk laundry detergent—now deceased. Every year, surveys indicated that women throughout the [United States] hated, abhorred the commercials. Yet every year, Wisk continued to move off the shelves, maintaining and even increasing market share. Guilt equaled a search for perfection, publicly denied, privately embraced."

Lyndsay Michaels, who works in marketing in the United Kingdom, wrote, "Dove, I think, skims along this fine edge and (generally) promotes the comforting message of 'Hey, look: Here's a product that might help you get a little nearer to your ideal, but, y'know, if you don't immediately (or ever) transform into a top supermodel, then that's just fine!' This is the same kind of supportive message I'd get from my best friends, rather than the adolescent, locker-room, two-faced bitchiness that other ads seem to emulate. I'm not saying I believe Dove without question, but that approach is so refreshing in these cynical times that it does stand out from the crowd. It is therefore often held up as an example of what the future could hold if ad makers and the general media were a bit less aggressive and manipulative. Personally, I'd love to see things progress further in that direction, for both sexes. I think it's high time to stop using our fears and perceived inadequacies as triggers to purchase, and start developing a more positive approach to our basic human desire to improve ourselves and our surroundings. Happily, I think we are moving that way, albeit gradually. I just hope we can keep the momentum going until it becomes the norm."

Sarah Freas, a marketing manager and blogger in Massachusetts, wrote, "What of the reality shows? Perfection? No way. *American Idol* and *Dancing with the Stars*? No perfection there. *The Daily Show* succeeds in laughing at all our imperfections. The problem with the attainment of perfect beauty is it's transitory. The perfection of the adeptly applied eyeliner ceases to exist once the brush is lifted from the eyelid. Perspiration enters the pores and, oops, the perfect graphic quality is lost. We are a global population on the move. Perfection in beauty ended when the salons of the drawing rooms of late closed their doors. Just as was mentioned earlier regarding 'ring around the collar' ads, housewives purchased the detergent regardless of the fact that they hated the ad. Unless an ad is artfully produced and provides some entertainment value, most products promising perfection are purchased not because of the ad, but in spite of it."

T. J. Swafford, who on Soflow calls himself "T. J. 'I told you so' Swafford," challenged Freas and wrote, "Are you telling me that Rosie O'Donnell could easily be a spokesperson for Dove?" Freas retorted, "Absolutely, T. J., and what fun scripting and directing the ad!"

I had started quite the debate. Swafford, true to his nickname, wrote back, "LMAO [Laughing My Ass Off]. . . . Well, I tell you what, Sarah, you can center your entire Dove campaign around ole Rosie (best of luck with the 'shower/tub' scene). . . . I'll center mine around Demi Moore and her *much* younger husband and we'll let the chips fall where they will. Talk about 'fun scripting and directing the ad.' Wanna bet Demi has more pull? Figuratively *and* literally. Sexy as all hell *and* funny to boot? . . . Killer combination in my books. Too bad we could [not] have a competition like this. . . . I think it would be fun to have all of you review the campaign's pros and cons."

I decided it was time to add my two cents. I wrote, "I've interviewed many women, and universally everyone loves Dove. That kind of consensus is rare. When I ask women about advertising, they have so many different opinions (and they love and hate ads for a million different reasons). They all loved Dove, and with such gusto. But I was surprised to learn that only some of them actually bought Dove products. . . . So I think women say they like the Dove brand (and they probably do like Dove's message), but when it comes to buying the product, women are more influenced by the aspiration message. And isn't that why we buy cosmetics in the first place? If we all thought we were beautiful, we wouldn't need the new firming cream or lipstick."

That being said, I explained that I didn't think T. J. Swafford was correct that Demi Moore would be a slam-dunk success. Because we are living in an era of reality, I believe that today's women respond to ads that show more realistic images. The feminist movement has also made its mark. It's made women want more from their beauty icons. Women want them to also be genuine and some combination of smart, witty, talented, and feisty. I wrote, "I think we're smart enough to know that if Demi Moore is selling me lipstick and I buy it, I did that in part because I want to be like her. And I actually don't want to just be gorgeous. . . . I'd be more inclined to put my consumer faith in a woman like Jennifer Hudson, Lisa Ling, Tina Fey, or Naomi Judd. These women are themselves in the public eye. They've shared a larger slice of their life with America—their humor, their insights, a life-changing story, or their greatest triumph. Their physical beauty is just one part of what makes them fabulous (and it's not the prevailing reason they are famous). They are attainably pretty (i.e., I could look like them on my best day), but more important, they are talented, smart, courageous, and they talk like real people. These women lend legitimacy to a product. If they say the firming cream works, I believe it. And I don't feel shallow when I buy the product."

While many of the women I spoke to told me that they didn't buy Dove products, the reality is that women on the whole are in love with Dove. The company's sales have grown tremendously since the launch of the Campaign for Real Beauty. The research firm Information Resources, Inc. (IRI) has reported that in 2006, sales increased 10.1 percent, to $589.2 million. In 2005, sales increased by 12.5 percent. In 2004, sales increased by just 2 percent, though that small increase is likely because the campaign launched near the end of 2004.[10] Dove's sales also rose in 2007, but just barely, according to IRI. Some in the industry have speculated that consumers didn't take to Dove's Pro-Age ads and its line of products for older women. However, a Dove spokesman told *Advertising Age* that 2007 sales are growing in the important body-wash category.[11] IRI derives the sales figures by collecting and totaling sales data from grocery stores, drugstores, and big-box stores like Target and Kmart, except for Wal-Mart, which doesn't share its sales figures with IRI.

These numbers were surprisingly difficult to find because Dove has been tight-lipped about its sales. Kathy O'Brien, Dove's marketing director, wouldn't reveal sales numbers in our interview. In 2005, in an interview with *USA Today,* she would say only that the company was "definitely meeting expectations of what we thought the campaign would do."[12]

I don't understand that. Dove, the catalyst of this movement, a company that claims to care about changing the face of advertising for women, should tout its sales figures—shout them from the rooftops. It would show other companies that sales don't necessarily suffer if the message of unattainable perfection is abandoned.

While much of the public may not be aware of Dove's success, it is likely that many in the business community are aware, due to reports from IRI and similar firms that monitor sales figures for large companies like Dove. However, it's possible that these companies may view Dove's success as a fluke, since the brand was the first to make such a bold statement, and believe that any company using the same approach would see less powerful results, because the antiperfection message is no longer fresh. Certainly, it would be risky to copycat Dove's campaign, but in this new era of TiVo and fragmentation, everything is risky. The fine-as-you-are message could be re-created in new ways and is worth a try.

Dove's bold step for womankind could turn out to be either the start of a small footnote in advertising history or the beginning of a major shift in female-targeted advertising. In the end, the ones who have the power to create that shift are today's mindful female consumers—the ones who buy from companies that treasure them—as well as brave marketers willing to risk the bottom line. To win the hearts, minds, and money of today's women, the dream boats of the advertising world need to check their egos at the door, throw caution to the wind, and put Plain Jane and Ugly Betty on their arm.

CHAPTER 7

The Romantic

The romantic picks the best restaurants, sends flowers, and writes beautiful love letters, telling his girl that she deserves only the very best. He massages her shoulders. Tells her she is working too hard.

Companies romance their female consumers by whispering the same sweet nothings. They say their products are the best, the most luxurious, and for only the most discriminating customers. Products are marketed as indulgences that women have earned, and, in their ever-hectic lives, it's no wonder so many women buy into that message.

Perhaps the most popular commercial to capitalize on the pampering pledge was Coty's Calgon bubble bath. The famous "Calgon, take me away" commercial showed a stressed-out housewife who utters those famous words and is immediately shown in a frothy, worry-free bubble bath. Since that commercial ran in the 1980s, the phrase "Calgon, take me away" has become part of our vernacular. The slogan resonated with overworked and stressed-out women who were juggling work and home, and welcomed the suggestion that they treat themselves to something special.

Women's marketing expert and writer Holly Buchanan told me that the pampering pledge is a little different today. "They've tweaked it into rejuvenation," Buchanan said, explaining that pampering used to be something women did only after they surpassed their stress limit, which automatically tied negative feelings to the concept of pampering (as in the case of the Calgon commercials). Today's pampering is more about being proactive and holistic. "It's more about taking care and building back energy; it's more of a health-and-wellness twist," Buchanan said. Clearly, the women's gym chain Curves got the message. A 2007 commercial told women, "You deserve thirty minutes of your own time. Thirty to recharge. Thirty to get a little boost. Thirty minutes on the Curves circuit to motivate your mind and your body, with the help of trainers who care and are always there to help you stay on track. Take thirty and get a total body workout with our total support."

Kraft followed the rejuvenation trend with ads for its salad dressings. A print ad for Kraft's Asian Toasted Sesame salad dressing showed a woman meditating in a yoga pose next to a salad and chopsticks. The ad read, "Rachel's Zen Asian salad."

Buchanan and many other trendspotters agree that Americans are beginning to value a more simplified, spiritual, "one with nature" way of life as a means of coping with today's fast-paced world. Buchanan described the new inner monologue many women are having as, *There must be something else out there. My life is more than shuttling the kids back and forth and going to work. My life has more meaning than this.*

It's become quite common to see commercials showing people in tense situations who are then soothed by the product being advertised. In a commercial for Airwick's plug-in air fresheners, a stressed-out woman is shown coming home from work, walking down a busy street while on her cell phone. When she opens the door of her apartment, she kicks off her pumps, plugs the Airwick air freshener into an electrical outlet, and retreats to a Zenlike room where imaginary rose petals float around her. The voice-over says, "Relax with Airwick's new relaxation-scented oil. With select essential oils like lavender and chamomile, it will give your home a special atmosphere of extraordinary well-being."

Stacey, age thirty, remembers being compelled to buy Häagen-Dazs ice cream after the company ran commercials that focused on the simplicity of the product. "It showed a rainforest with nuts dropping from the sky. It was very Zen. It was like, 'Pure vanilla,'" Stacey said in a very relaxing tone. "It was emphasizing the purity of the product. It was a very beautiful ad and very Zen, [implying] that eating ice cream is very natural and in touch."

In a recent ad for Yoplait Chocolate Whips, two women lounge at a day spa, wearing plush white robes. As they eat the airy chocolate mousse from the Yoplait container, they trade flowery descriptions of how good the yogurt is. Here's a basic transcript:

WOMAN 1: "This is, like, Zen-wrapped-in-karma-dipped-in-chocolate good."

WOMAN 2: "Soaking-in-a-chocolate-bath good."

WOMAN 1: "No, a-head-to-toe-chocolate-body-wrap good."

WOMAN 2: "Getting-a-foot-massage-while-shoe-shopping . . . "

WOMAN 1: " . . . for-chocolate-covered-heels good."

MALE VOICE-OVER: "Introducing Yoplait's oh-so-indulgent chocolate mousse Whips. It is so good."

In another example, a July 2007 commercial for the GMC Acadia, a crossover vehicle (which imparts qualities of an SUV and a car), took a luxurious tack. The black-and-white ad shows two young beautiful girls on a shopping expedition. One of the girls is driving, while her friend rides along. They both wear scarves in their hair and glamorous oversize black sunglasses. The two rows of seats behind them are full of shopping bags. The voice-over says, "With room for up to eight . . . or two best friends and seventy-five shopping bags . . . the GMC Acadia is one stylish shopping cart. You can see the stunning crossover this summer in the Hamptons at Super Saturday, the fashion fundraiser for ovarian cancer research. Preview it now online."

The Super Saturday event is held annually in Bridgehampton. Clothing from top fashion designers is on sale there at discount prices, with proceeds benefiting ovarian cancer research. However, the high-class event requires tickets, which cost $400 each. By linking itself to the Hamptons event and showing the glamorous, shopaholic commercial, GMC spoke to women who couldn't afford a $38,000 Lexus or BMW crossover vehicle, but could afford the Acadia and wanted a car that is associated with luxury.

Chocolate is commonly marketed with the indulgence pitch. Case in point: a commercial for Betty Crocker Warm Delights, a single-serving chocolate brownie dessert that just needs to be warmed up in the microwave. As sultry music wafts in the background, the camera slowly pans through a girl's urban loft. We see her keys and wallet on the counter and her shoes lying in the middle of the hallway. She has gotten home from work and lies on her sofa, indulging in the warm, gooey brownie as we hear a female voice-over say, "Now Betty can melt away your entire day in just three minutes. Introducing Betty Crocker Warm Delights. In delicious molten caramel cake and decadent hot fudge brownie. For a taste of delight, you're just three minutes from heaven."

Though many women dream of relaxing at a day spa or unwinding on a Friday night at a five-star restaurant that serves chocolate soufflé, the reality is that most have mortgages, credit card bills, and children, which prevent them from booking that massage. They don't have the time or money to indulge, though they really want and need to. That's where Yoplait, Kraft, and Betty Crocker come in.

Retail strategist and futurist Candace Corlett, from the firm WSL Strategic Retail, told me that consumer products companies have also ponied up with at-home beauty kits, facial peels, highlighting kits, and teeth-whitening strips. "Think about the bath market. For years the message was 'taking the time behind a closed door in the bathroom and having a bath.' And advertisers finally gave up on that and created the shower gel, so all that relaxing ambience of a bath, in terms of fragrance and skin benefits, is accomplished in a three-minute shower," she said.

Calgon is one of the only brands in the bath/shower category that has been around long enough to experience the shift from long bath to quick shower. Sure enough, when I went to the company website, I saw that Calgon had shifted its focus away from its iconic bubble bath. There was much more emphasis on its new body mists, lotions, and body washes. Quick, indulgent products have become popular, Corlett said, because more "time-consuming indulgences" aren't a reality for most mainstream women. Instead, time-consuming indulgences are a notion women are aware of. They know they should take time out for themselves and unwind in meditative ways, though they actualize that message in their own more attainable ways. "They're doing it with a new skin cream line from Johnson & Johnson," Corlett said, giving me one example. "And it amounts to skin cream that you apply and breathe deeply while applying. I don't see [women] living the message. I see them buying products that acknowledge that they are aware of the message, but they aren't living the message. It's about time. They don't have the time," she said.

Brawny gets the award for selling women the most nonindulgent product with a pampering pledge. The company produced a reality show at a private camp in the mountains (named the Brawny Academy), where men are trained to become better mates to their wives and girlfriends. Their trials and travails were recorded and produced in a series of episodes, also called "webisodes," which ran on the Brawny website.

The handsome actor who plays the Brawny Man was the host of the show. In the first show, he walked into the frame (carrying an ax) and addressed the camera kindly, saying, "You know there is nothing like chopping wood to the sound of the red-throated boiler to make you realize what's important—like being a dependable, strong, yet caring man. That's just what we teach at Brawny Academy. Today, eight men are being sent here by the women in their lives to learn these very qualities. I'm going to help them become more thoughtful, more helpful, even more romantic. My goal is that they leave as changed men, better men."

Throughout the remainder of the webisodes, the men were put through challenges designed to reform them, making them more sensitive and caring to the women in their lives. Naturally, there was an ample supply of Brawny paper towels on hand to help them along the way. In the final episode, the new-and-improved men hosted their ladies at the academy, reading them poems and serving them a black-tie dinner. It ended with the men being interviewed, explaining all they learned from the Brawny Academy.

One man said, "I think the Brawny Man represents who we are and who we can be inside. If we can be more like him overall as a person, then maybe we'll be a better husband, a better spouse, a better father for ourselves and for our families in the future." Another man said, "Working at Brawny Camp, I was clueless, unromantic, and just really disrespectful to my girlfriend. After going through the academy, I see where I need to change, and I want to go home with the attitude and the gung-ho to get it done." After the finale, viewers were invited to vote on who they believed was the most improved man.

It's not easy to apply an indulgence or pampering message to paper towels, but Brawny, its parent company, Georgia-Pacific, and its marketing firm Fallon, found a way. They turned the concept on its head and gained more Brawny buyers by capitalizing on the popularity of the Brawny Man, a character who represents the perfect man—one who not only can chop wood, but who also cares about a clean kitchen.

To learn more about the Brawny Academy, I called up Derek Schwendinger, the brand manager for towel strategy at Georgia-Pacific (yes, that's a real title). He told me that the company produced the webisodes as a way to create an emotional connection with its target consumers, moms between the ages of 25 and 54 who are "passionate about homekeeping." Schwendinger explained that there is loyalty in the paper towel category of consumer products. Some consumers are willing to pay full price for a high-quality paper towel brand. In the biz, these consumers are called "category passionates." Brawny was looking for more of them.

One of Brawny's goals was to show consumers that its product was not just a strong paper towel, but was also versatile. Schwendinger said that the company had conducted focus groups beforehand, and had asked women what words they associated with Brawny paper towels. Most women thought of strength first. While strength is a positive quality, Schwendinger said, the company was concerned about the brand's one-dimensionality. Brawny also wondered if strength alone had negative overtones, countering positive qualities like softness and absorbency. The company couldn't deny that its webisodes were a risk, likely being the first time a company had marketed a product through an online reality show. However, considering the current advertising and consumer landscape, Georgia-Pacific felt it was a risk worth taking. "With cost and fragmentation, anyone would tell you that it's harder and harder to reach your consumer effectively," Schwendinger said.

Research showed that the web was a safe bet, since it is such a popular hangout for women. "Certainly, we had the stats behind the number of women who are gaming, getting online, spending time online. It lined up well with what we were trying to achieve," he said. Beforehand, Brawny put on its scholar hat and hired an outside firm to conduct what Schwendinger called "qualitative in-home ethnographic research," where a researcher goes into the homes of consumers to observe a typical day. One of the most consistent findings was that women wanted more help from their mates with housekeeping duties.

"Women who were married or had a significant other said they were disappointed with the lack of contribution from the men in their lives," Schwendinger said. That research reminded me of a report I came across from the marketing firm Euro RSCG. That survey found that massive numbers of women were fed up with their husbands. As mentioned in chapter one ("The Scholar"), the marketing firm labeled these women the Rage Brigade, describing them as women who work outside the home and take on most of the household responsibilities, thus feeling rage toward their husbands for not making more money and not helping out more around the house.

Georgia-Pacific was not familiar with the Euro RSCG survey when it launched the webisodes, Schwendinger said. Brawny's research found that women weren't exactly enraged; they were just hoping their husbands would contribute around the house more. In a quest to help women live that ideal online, Georgia-Pacific set out to redefine the über-strong Brawny Man, making him a Renaissance man who could teach other men to follow his lead, cooking gourmet food, writing poetry, and cleaning the kitchen. Not only would it show the softer side of the brand, it would also show female consumers that the Brawny brand cares about them and believes they deserve better from their mates.

Approximately 400,000 people viewed each of the webisodes of the show, Schwendinger said. Altogether, the site was visited more than 850,000 times. Each web visit, on average, lasted more than thirteen minutes, a phenomenal amount of time considering that few people today can get through a thirty-second commercial.

After airing the webisodes, Brawny hired a research company to survey viewers. The research company asked viewers whether they thought Brawny was a brand that supports women. Viewers answered yes to that question 150 percent more than nonviewers did, Schwendinger said. Viewers were asked whether the Brawny Man and Brawny paper towels were versatile. Viewers answered yes to that question 47 percent more than nonviewers. Purchase intent was up 52 percent among webisode viewers. Sales were also up about 10 percent.

"I don't know that we would've had the same kind of engagement running more thirty-second spots," Schwendinger said, referring to television commercials. Georgia-Pacific is strongly considering a second season of the Brawny Academy, though the compnay later ended its relationship with Fallon. I wrote Brawny and asked them why, but never got a response.

When I asked a few women what they thought of the concept, most reacted positively. "Is this for real?" one woman asked me. "I think it is hilarious! My husband could use a trip there!" thirtysomething wife and mom Andrea told me. Twenty-five-year-old Jackie, from Philadelphia, hadn't heard of the Brawny Academy until I told her about it. After going to the Brawny website and checking out the online reality show, she was intrigued. And she could see why other women, wives in particular, would appreciate the show's premise. "It made me feel that Brawny is a brand that puts a lot of time into trying to reach their customers, but it didn't make me feel like I have to buy Brawny paper towels. I will probably continue to pick up whatever brand of paper towels are the cheapest." Jackie said she would never splurge on paper towels, even if she was wooed by the Brawny Man. He had little effect on her, because she's quite happy with her husband. "My husband does a pretty good job around the house. Of course, there are things I wish he would do better, like clean up his video games better or put away his shoes, but it's not like he would ever give me a bow and arrow as a gift. So I think the episodes might have had more of an impact on me if I had a husband like some of those guys," she said.

Although Jackie couldn't be romanced by Brawny, other brands have convinced her to splurge. Her most recent purchase was a high-end golf club, the Nike SasQuatch driver, which she said has given her more confidence on the course, because not only is the driver carried by many experienced golfers on her course, but it is also used by Tiger Woods. "When I walk up to the tee, it looks like I belong on that course. That comes, big-time, from insecurity, because I'm an okay golfer, but I'm probably not even approaching good. But I care about my appearance. I blend in easier," she told me. But usually when Jackie splurges, it is on little things, like a pricier shampoo. "I can remember the Herbal Essences from high school. It was the shampoo that all the girls, myself included, wanted. It was considered indulgent," she said, adding that she still buys that brand now. "It feels more relaxing to shampoo with my $3.79 Herbal Essences than it does with my $0.99 Suave. It's more of a treat."

Thirty-five-year-old Phoenix mom Jen told me that she's also come to find indulgence in little things, like the smell of eucalyptus in the aerobics room at her gym, and in little purchases at the grocery store, where she often selects food that has the most attractive packaging, rather than looking only at the price. "I'm picking out chicken nuggets for the kids, and there are a couple different brands. But I picked the one where the chicken looks the best," she said, laughing, as if realizing that her comment might sound silly. "It's the little indulgences that make you happy."

Steve Castle, a luxury consultant and the former editor of the national high-end magazine *The Robb Report,* told me that indulgence has always been a very powerful marketing tool, although companies can sometimes focus too much on the attributes of the product and not enough on the experience of buying and using the product. "To fully understand this, one has to start by realizing that luxury is not a thing, but an experience."

Professor and author James Twitchell, who has studied and written about the history of indulgence in social culture, said that in the thirteenth century, the Roman Catholic Church began selling indulgences to people, essentially promising them a speedier route to heaven in exchange for their money. Therefore, by purchasing an indulgence, people were attaining a higher status in heaven. A similar ideal applies today. By indulging in a luxury item, such as a Louis Vuitton handbag, a BMW, or a Viking stove, we are telling other people that we are of a higher social class.

Throughout the twentieth century, consumers of all social classes have acquired more luxury goods, making high-end designer brands household names. Various changes in the business world and popular culture have made this a reality. Twitchell explained that advertisers were able to convince consumers that luxury brands are worth the expense, even though the products are relatively interchangeable with competing mainstream brands. Most consumers understand this, though many still prefer the luxury brand as a means to propel them up the social ladder. Also, because of sophisticated advertising and manufacturing machinery in the twentieth century, companies were able to mass-produce items that had previously taken more time to create, such as cars, leather goods, and watches. That led to the formation of heritage brands, like Louis Vuitton, Coach, BMW, and Rolex.

The American standard of living also improved dramatically during the second half of the twentieth century. Luxury market consultant and author Pam Danziger explained that in the post–World War II period, the United States saw the emergence of the middle class. At that time, Americans were buying products that made life more comfortable. "We saw lots of purchases on products and services that upped our standard of living," Danziger said. These included goods like washers, dryers, televisions, air conditioners, and refrigerators. As the decades wore on, the middle class acquired all of these basic comfort items and then turned its attention to luxury items that were once reserved only for the rich. "So now, the bump is to a plasma screen TV," Danziger said. "That is only an incremental step [compared with] the big development that was radio to TV."

Luxury goods have become so appealing that middle-class consumers are buying them even when they don't have the discretionary funds. Twitchell said the business world tapped into this irrational yearning by developing financing programs so that the middle class could taste a bit more of the sweet life. "We have systems to have something like the Lexus car. But instead of being able to afford it, you can lease it. Instead of having a vacation *casita,* you can have a time-share. With frequent flyer miles, you get upgraded to first class," he said. "[The middle class] can have it, but they just can't have it for long, and they can't have a lot of it." This pattern is referred to in the business world as the "down-marketing" of luxury.

Castle believes this down-marketing has made luxury brands very rich. "There's a saying: 'Sell to the wealthy, live with the masses; sell to the masses, live with the wealthy,'" he said. Between the middle class and the wealthy lies a growing number of people who are considered "mass affluent." The U.S. Census Bureau defines the "mass affluent" as people with household incomes over $75,000. In 1980, 15 percent of U.S. households were mass affluent (in 2003 adjusted dollars). In 2003, that figure was up to 26 percent.[1]

The mass affluent, or what Castle calls the "wannabes," are the hungriest for luxury goods. "They happen to be in very competitive positions in their businesses and social structures with other mass affluent wannabes. Think status is important to many people? Now put a lot of money in front of them as well. I argue that for many wannabes, status is never more important than it is when they are in this income bracket and striving to get into the next. Many here feel the acute need to have the car, the house, and other items that don't merely signify their upper-middle-class positions, but cast them as attaining the next level among their peers."

This is especially true for female consumers, according to women's studies professor Jennifer Scanlon, who has studied the trajectory of advertising. She told me that an argument can be made that luxury goods have replaced men as the thing women use to demonstrate their status. As thirty-one-year-old Phoenix executive and mom Nicole told me, "It's part quality, part the expectation on where you are. You are making a statement.

It sounds so bad, but there is a level of expectation." Nicole often carries a designer handbag into meetings with corporate partners. "They expect us to look and talk a certain way and have certain things," she told me. "Maybe it makes me feel like I'm more prepared when I see them, even though it has nothing to do with my skills. But it does play into my overall confidence." Nicole's brand of choice is the leather goods maker Coach. However, she told me that she doesn't buy the high-end handbags for status alone. She also sees them as a way of rewarding herself. She even displays her many Coach bags neatly in her closet, like trophies in a case.

Another woman, thirty-year-old Andrea, told me she carries a knock-off Coach bag that everyone thinks is real. I asked her why she wanted it. "It was the society thing. Everyone else had it, so why couldn't I look like I had one? It's super cute. I get compliments on it every single day. I feel good that I do carry it, whether I look like crap that day or not. People automatically identify with it. They are like, 'Where did you get your Coach?' No one ever complimented my black bag from Ross."

On the grand scale, the middle class and upper-middle class are hungry for luxury items, but the economy can cause the buying wave to ebb in small spurts of time. Retail strategist and futurist Candace Corlett, from the firm WSL Strategic Retail, explained that while middle-income customers bought more luxury items in the late '90s and throughout the first few years of the new millennium, their splurging declined beginning in 2005. "Certainly, there was this sense throughout 1998 to 2004 that everybody is entitled to a little bit of affluence, to a taste of luxury," Corlett explained. "You know, if you couldn't afford a Donna Karan coat, you could afford her belt or bag. We used to say, 'Everybody wants a little bit of Donna.' We saw the young girls walking around with Prada or Gucci bags. The headlines were full of it. Now we're seeing headlines about budget stores."

In our interview, Corlett explained that WSL Strategic Retail's most recent "How America Shops" annual report showed that the middle class is shopping more like lower-income customers in an effort to save money. This is due in part to a delayed reaction to the dot-com bust, 9/11, falling interest rates, and collapsing corporations like Enron and WorldCom. "And while those companies may have impacted a very small percentage of the population, the impact is, *It's Enron one day and WorldCom the next. It could happen to me,*" she said.

In our interview, Corlett pointed out JCPenney, saying that the company smartly took note of the change in economic climate, rolling out more designer lines at affordable prices "to take that woman who, in the '90s, felt she was entitled to luxury, and [make] her reentry into reality a bit easier," she said.

Like JCPenney, Sears is a midtier department store. In 2006, a Sears commercial reached for middle-income customers with an indulgence message that promoted its holiday sale. The commercial showed a woman putting her three children back in their car seats after a day of shopping. It doesn't look like easy work, but this woman appears to be in control as she maneuvers bags, jackets, and whiny kids. As we watch her, we hear the voice-over say,

"Is this the face of a shopping novice? Someone scared by a 'Hurry, sale ends soon'? This is a woman who can buy four thoughtful gifts in ten minutes. A woman who can emerge from a candy aisle candy-free. A woman who can change a diaper inside a snowsuit. This is a woman who deserves a little gravy for just gettin' out there. Don't miss the big 50-percent-off sale."

After being blindsided by edgy ads, disheartened by sex-laden ads, and annoyed by loud, obnoxious ads, many women appreciate the gentle, sweet, "you deserve it" message that comes from the romantic. After all, when they aren't dodging marketing messages, many women are multitasking, juggling more duties than ever, with little time for themselves. They welcome the soothing virtual shoulder massage that comes in an ad for Brawny, Yoplait, or Betty Crocker. They also appreciate being courted by high-priced designer brands that previously were reserved for the affluent. They are wooed by Tiffany's line of sterling silver jewelry that costs less than $500 per piece, Coach's $300 handbags, and Lexus's leases. Luxury brands and perks are now accessible to all, creating new standards and competition among middle-class consumers who often can't afford these products but are tempted by them every day. Many are delving into considerable debt. By some estimates, the average American household has $9,000 in credit card debt.

The pampering pledge in advertising has normalized luxury to the point that many consumers feel entitled to it and simply can't resist. And it's made some women quite vulnerable to the romantic, who, in the end, isn't actually doing her any favors.

CHAPTER 8

The Sneak

The sneak always has a trick up his sleeve. When he's chasing a woman, he bribes a few friends to drop his name into conversations with her. Or he adjusts his schedule so that he crosses her path more often, though he acts as if each encounter is a coincidence.

Marketers are finding that they, too, need to sneak around to better reach consumers. A growing number of consumers are ignoring traditional advertising and are automatically rejecting products that come with blatant sales pitches or appear to be too corporate. In 2004, Howard Handler, the chief marketing officer at Virgin Mobile, told the media that young people in particular have developed sensitive marketing filters because they "have been completely surrounded by media since the day they were born." He added that "they let in the things that are authentic, and everything else they ignore."[1]

Camille, a twenty-three-year-old New Yorker, is one of those young people Handler described: skeptical of advertising and in search of authenticity. Camille is disillusioned by corporate America, dislikes traditional advertising, and is skeptical of what big business perpetuates. She sometimes refers to corporate America as "the man," and she thinks that celebrities who star in advertisements are corporate shills. Camille prefers to learn about new products from her friends, as well as from blogs and podcasts, because she considers them to be pure, unbiased sources of information. "[Friends] have no other motivation than to help you. They aren't making any money. And there are so many products in this ongoing state of capitalism. There is this onslaught of products that say they are all better than another," she said. "They are all gunning for your money, and not for your betterment."

Camille admits she has little money for companies to gun for. She lives in Brooklyn in a one-bedroom apartment she shares with a friend. Camille sleeps in the living room. With aspirations to work in the music business, she is currently a receptionist at a music firm, paying her dues. As she walks to work each morning, she uses a kind of radar for advertising messages. Most of the time, Camille can find a way to debunk all of the billboard messages she sees, deeming them inauthentic.

Because consumers so often ignore ads or cynically deconstruct them, companies are replacing traditional advertising with public relations, product placement, and word-of-mouth strategies to sneak up on consumers without hitting them over the head with sales pitches. The examples are varied, creative, and endless in number. Toyota's Scion brand partnered with two streetwear clothing designers to create an urban golf clothing line called Release. Heineken started a podcast on the web that tied rock music to its beer. Procter & Gamble's CoverGirl cosmetics brand made a deal with Running Press, a unit of Perseus Books Group, to mention its Lipslicks lipstick in a fiction book aimed at adolescent girls.[2] Magazines such as *Domino* and *Lucky* function more like catalogs, pairing photos of new styles with captions that tell readers the brand, price, and website where the products can be purchased.

Product placement has also become a common occurrence on television. *American Idol* judges sip from Coca-Cola cups. *America's Next Top Model* contestants wear CoverGirl makeup and compete to become CoverGirl's newest spokesmodel. *Project Runway* designers scurry to the Macy's accessories suite and the L'Oréal makeup room before testing their dresses on the runway. Giveaways have become commonplace on morning and afternoon chat shows such as *The View, Ellen,* and *Oprah,* as the host tells the audience they are winning a new gadget, cosmetic, or appliance, causing the audience to erupt in cheers as viewers at home are forced to hear the advertising shpiel about the product being given away. Other companies pay to have their products stuffed in swag bags that are given out to celebrities at Hollywood events, in hopes that a Julia Roberts or Reese Witherspoon will discover the item and then be photographed and featured in magazines wearing or using their product. Brands are making their products more identifiable, so that people can easily see if a bystander is using, say, an iPhone, a Verizon Chocolate cell phone, or a Cingular Red Pearl cell phone. Food companies such as Mars, Kraft, and PepsiCo are even testing out scent technology to spread the aroma of their products into the air of shopping centers. Talk about sneaky.

Gary Ruskin, from the consumer advocacy group Commercial Alert, is concerned about these methods and the overall advertising landscape. His group works to keep advertising in what he calls "its proper sphere." That's a tall order. Ruskin believes that companies began overstepping marketing bounds in the 1970s and '80s, as the government gave businesses more constitutional speech protections. Over the past three decades, corporations have gained more and more power to advertise wherever and whenever they want. "That's the legal underpinning for 'ad creep,'" Ruskin said, defining the term as "the ability for the advertisers to hang a jingle under our eyes anytime they want." Ad creep has also flourished because television commercials have lost their oomph. "By all accounts, the thirty-second spot is declining in effectiveness," Ruskin said—something I heard umpteen times throughout my reporting. "That means advertisers need new ways to get their messages out. What used to be focused like a laser beam, via the TV set to people in their homes, now has become diffused throughout the culture. That has been a principal reason why we see ads in so many parts of our culture."

Of all of the types of ad creep, product placement on television concerns Ruskin the most. "The reason is, it's so effective. There is not very much data on it, but what data we have is very alarming," he said. Of that data, one study revealed that half of all teenagers who smoke begin the habit because they saw it in a television show or movie, Ruskin said.

While most of the characters smoking in movies aren't doing so because a tobacco company has paid for its placement, this statistic proves that when a product is shown in a movie or on television, it tremendously influences its audience. Ruskin believes this is why we've seen an explosion in product placement over the past ten years: "because it works so well. It sneaks past our critical faculties when we are paying less attention, and implants its message in our brains."

Ruskin believes that companies have created their own nightmare, flooding the marketplace with ad creep that has diluted the overall strength of marketing. "In order for advertising to work these days, they have to do the new intrusive thing, and then the next day it's the new *new* intrusive thing. And so there is this increasing intrusiveness in order to get attention," he told me. This trend, for example, is happening online. The Pew Research Center has found that spam has reduced the effectiveness of online advertising: 25 percent of email users said they use email less because of spam, and 52 percent trust email less because of it.

This intrusiveness has Camille and many other consumers on the defense. "I think my generation has such a mistrust of being sold anything. We buy and buy as much as anything else, and it feels dirty," she said. "The times we live in, you know, the politicians that lie. These are cynical times. My generation is living in a time when there is access to information that has debunked a lot of crap, so the hard part is finding things that are true and good and reliable."

Because mass corporate brands are often seen as less cool and more evil than smaller, independent ones, companies are linking up with new pop culture icons, such as free-spirited bloggers, antiestablishment artists, and trend writers who have street credibility in the cool department. Camille calls people like this "tastemakers" and said she frequently sees companies trying to get their products in the hands of these influencers.

The website Daily Candy is a key tastemaker that Camille values. The free Daily Candy email service gives subscribers (I am one of them) a daily dose of information on new products, stores, and trends. In an email, Camille told me, "I appreciate Daily Candy because it's well written and, though they are honest that they are trying to get you to buy stuff, they 1) seem not to be such corporate shills; rather, it seems they are (at least in my mind) a group of stylish girls who are suggesting products they would actually use and places they actually go, and 2) aren't always trying to get you to buy stuff. Sometimes they will just recommend something you should see or just talk about a new social trend." This kind of inside information is what keeps Camille ahead of the trends. "I'm interested in finding something off the beaten path," she told me. "With so many choices out there, it helps to have someone you like and trust cut through all the noise."

On the opposite side of the country, in Los Angeles, thirty-year-old Stacey told me she also relies on Daily Candy for information about products, brands, and services, because she too prefers the path less traveled by consumers. "I'd like to think that I'm part of this elite group that knows about stuff," she said, explaining that she is more inclined to buy something when she has heard about it from an e-newsletter, *The New Yorker* magazine, or from a friend, as opposed to a commercial on a major broadcast network. "Mass advertising has less of a direct effect on me, because it seems like everyone is doing it. I don't want to buy what everyone else is buying. I'd like to think of myself as special. And I also don't have a lot of money, so it's not like I can go to Rome and buy a handbag for $8,000. So this is my way around that. I can still feel exclusive, but it's also in my budget," she said. "If I could, I'd buy all my clothes at Prada, but I can't. So you read about the little designer on Daily Candy, and it's more in the realm of the possible."

Still, Laura, thirty-six and from Brooklyn, told me that Daily Candy is losing its independent cachet. "Originally it started as a friend telling you a secret in your ear, and it has evolved into a commercial. I'm actually looking at it right now, and there's an advertisement for Aveeno in the corner. They are working in banner ads." Laura signed up for Daily Candy for the site's endorsement, or what she calls a "stamp of cool," for new products, services, and companies. "I don't mind that 'stamp of cool' for a one man–owned boutique or a restaurant that just opened, but I don't want that stamp on global corporate products."

While Camille didn't have the same skepticism about Daily Candy, she generally takes issue with most forms of marketing. She saw through a partnership struck between the Eastsport backpack company and the MisShapes DJs, three young New York City DJs who have become pop culture icons because of their über-cool parties. The MisShapes DJs were featured in an Eastsport backpack ad campaign that included a billboard Camille spotted while walking to work. She immediately viewed the MisShapes as "total shills. They seemed to be a very mismatched choice for the backpack company. They represent a particular nightlife culture very far removed from places where a backpack would be used," she said, adding, "In fact, you probably would not be let into any of their clubs were you carrying one of those things."

Camille, Stacey, and Laura realize that companies are also motivated to put products into *their* hands in particular. All three of these women could also be considered influencers or tastemakers by marketers, since they are young urbanites who frequent the art and music scenes, and since they prefer chic, noncorporatized products. "Being young and being in this city, you get a lot [for free], because they know that if you like it and you're a trusted cool kid, you'll spread the word," Camille said.

Bars in New York City frequently serve free drinks because a company sponsor has picked up the tab. Camille told me this happens so often that there is even a website that New York residents can access to learn which bars are offering company-sponsored drinks each weekend. She recently went "gallery hopping" around New York City to enjoy various types of art. "Some people go for the free alcohol," she said. "Once you get out there, you wander. You see people going in and out." Usually the free alcohol at galleries is a mere glass of wine. But in this most recent gallery-hop, Camille noticed that there was a larger offering of free alcohol being served, which she assumed was a marketing strategy. "There was a DJ and vanilla rum and cherry vodka, and yeah, we just kept drinking, and we were like, 'Wow, I've never drank that much at a gallery,'" she told me, laughing. "They must have been trying to market this cherry vodka." And Camille assumes that the folks marketing the cherry vodka wanted their products at art galleries to attract people like her. "I figured that someone must have thought, *This is a group of people who are cool, and if they like it, it must be cool too.*"

She remembers getting free stuff in college, which she assumes was given to her for the same reason. Later, while Camille was living in an art collective in New York, her roommate once came in the door with a case of Red Bull, a freebie randomly delivered to their doorstep from the company. Camille is happy to take advantage of free stuff, and often seeks out the bars that are offering sponsored drinks. However, she is adamant that those brands aren't buying her loyalty. She will take advantage of the free stuff, but she feels no obligation to buy it down the road.

Certainly, companies want cool kids like Camille to sample their products and spread the word. But word-of-mouth marketing techniques are often more sophisticated than free giveaways. Traditionally, word of mouth has been thought of as a natural phenomenon that happens on its own and can't be predicted or controlled by the business world. However, in the past decade, word-of-mouth marketing firms have created ways to spread information effectively. This niche in the marketing field has grown by leaps and bounds over the past decade—so much so that there is an umbrella organization for professionals devoted to this specialty, the Word of Mouth Marketing Association. WOMMA defines the practice as giving people a reason to talk about specific brands, products, and services, and making it easier for that kind of conversation to take place.

Research has also been developed that measures the effectiveness of word of mouth. One company created TalkTrack, which interviews a sampling of seven hundred teens and adults around the country each week, asking them about their conversations. TalkTrack has found that the average American mentions brand names more than fifty times each week during normal conversation, and that 62 percent of brand mentions are positive, while less than 10 percent are negative. This data is convincing marketers to try word of mouth. Jim Kite, research director at the media agency Starcom, which uses TalkTrack research, told the *Financial Times* that in the environment of DVRs and MySpace, "word of mouth becomes more important, and the Internet and the huge increase in use of social networks allows information to spread more quickly." Kite said his firm did not realize just how important word of mouth is until it evaluated the TalkTrack research, adding, "[We] are telling our clients that they should change their entire approach to communications planning and make word of mouth the focus of campaigns."[3]

Paul Rand is the CEO of Zocalo Group, a firm that specializes in word-of-mouth campaigns. *Zócalo* is a Spanish word used to describe town squares where people meet to chat and swap stories. Rand told me that consumers are embracing word-of-mouth marketing because of numerous shifts happening in today's culture. He explained that because an abundance of information is available on the web, consumers are looking for credible ways to sort it all out. The ease of the web has also led people to gather and share information at unprecedented levels. "Current stats are showing that more than 90 percent of Americans say they would much prefer a peer-to-peer recommendation than [one] in terms of advertising, an email initiative, or any other type of communication. Knowing the information is sent and passed on from someone they know and trust is really the most convincing way to get an endorsement," he said.

Most word-of-mouth marketing firms focus on putting their clients' products into the hands of the consumers who are enthusiastic about the hottest new products on the market. Some call these people "early adopters." Rand calls them "bees."

"They create the buzz that people talk about," he said, telling me that a bee is the person in your life most likely to say, "Have you tried the new blankety-blank?" Word-of-mouth marketing firms have recruited thousands of bees, who buzz about products in exchange for compensation. These bees usually are not compensated with money but instead receive free products, a steady supply of coupons, discounts, and product samples, and access to special events. Sometimes they also earn points from these firms, which can be redeemed for merchandise. The bees' methods vary. For example, they might linger in coffeehouses with a new tech gadget that they subtly show passersby. Or they might post positive feedback about a product on popular websites in exchange for coupons or access to clubs and parties.

Depending on the word-of-mouth marketing firm's policy, bees may or may not be required to disclose that they have a relationship with a company or marketing firm and are compensated. Companies that do not require disclosure are sometimes referred to as stealth marketing firms. The word-of-mouth marketing firm Tremor is one of these stealth firms. Run by Procter & Gamble, Tremor targets consumers in their teens and twenties. The young bees who buzz for Tremor promote both P&G products and products for other entertainment, fashion, music, food, and beauty companies that contract with Tremor. The firm's website states, "Freedom of speech is the driving principal [sic] of Tremor. Members are always encouraged to speak freely, whether positive or negative. Tremor never tells teens what to say. We want teens to be honest about products and services that they are introduced to through Tremor . . . no matter what their opinion." Since Tremor does not tell its bees what to say, it does not require them to disclose that they are part of this network. Certainly, as more consumers reject the sales-pitchy side of advertising, this covert type of marketing has its benefits. Consumers never realize that they are being sold to. They assume that friends and acquaintances have no vested interest in endorsing a product. But this form of marketing is certainly sneaky.

In 2004, *The New York Times* ran a story about word-of-mouth marketing. It explained that Tremor finds influential young people, including teenagers, through a screening process and then handpicks bees by isolating their psychological characteristics. The story went on: "The details of this are a secret, but as an example, [Tremor CEO Steve] Knox noted that most teenagers have 25 or 30 names on their instant-messaging 'buddy list,' whereas a Tremor member might have 150. Tremor recruits volunteers mostly through online advertisements and accepts only 10 or 15 percent of those who apply. The important thing, Knox said, is they are the right kind of kids—the connected, influential trend-spreading kind. Knox mentioned a focus group of Tremor kids in Los Angeles, where several teenagers showed up with business cards."[4]

The story included an interview with a bee for Tremor, eighteen-year-old Janet Onyenucheya from New York City, who was plucked by the company while in high school. "Onyenucheya gets free stuff from Tremor, and sometimes even a small check for taking surveys and participating in focus groups. She got to vote on the design for a T-shirt for the 10th anniversary of the Vans Warped Tour and for the design of a Crest toothbrush. This past July, she was invited to an advance viewing of two television shows, *Lost* and *Complete Savages,* at the Millennium screening room in downtown Manhattan. There were about 70 teenagers there, and pizza and sodas for everybody. Onyenucheya particularly loved *Lost.* 'When I came home,' she said, 'I immediately told my five closest friends, like: "Oh, my God, you just missed the greatest shows. I got to go down to the Millennium and saw a show called *Lost* and it was so good, and we have to watch it when it comes out." And I felt like I had the upper hand.'"[5]

When I told Camille about stealth marketing, she realized that she could no longer completely trust endorsements from friends or bloggers, which she had previously considered to be the last pure, corporate-free way to learn about new things. "The man" put an end to that. "You think you know who your friends are. I don't know. It's like a sci-fi nightmare," she told me. "Hearing about this makes me super paranoid. It makes you wary of making new friends. You know, is this my new friend or my new marketer? It sounds horrible." This reminded Camille of a friend who once tried to sell her Mary Kay cosmetics. "It's my friend and she is making money off it, so once money enters into the equation, you have to scrutinize [the product] more."

Had Camille gone to a back-yard barbeque in 2004, she might have been unknowingly sold on Al Fresco brand chicken sausage. Back then, Al Fresco sought the help of word-of-mouth marketing firm BzzAgent to help promote its gourmet sausage. Bees for BzzAgent were sent coupons to buy the gourmet chicken sausage at their local supermarket and bring the sausage to the next barbeque they attended. While attending the barbeque, the bees could talk about the product with friends, see if their friends liked the sausage, and then report those findings back to BzzAgent, which then relayed the information back to Al Fresco. BzzAgent's campaign boosted sales of Al Fresco sausage by 100 percent in some markets that season.[6] BzzAgent has worked with scores of companies to promote their brands and products, including Anheuser-Busch, Lee Jeans, Ralph Lauren, and DuPont.

BzzAgent spokesman Joe Chernov noted that companies use word of mouth to gather consumer feedback, not just spread awareness about products. In some cases, after receiving feedback from BzzAgent's bees, companies have altered their product's ingredients, packaging, or marketing. For example, in 2005, BzzAgent sent samples of a cream cheese–yogurt spread to selected participants. Feedback revealed that most people liked the blueberry flavor most and thought the size of the container was too small. As a result, the manufacturer created the product in a "family size" in the blueberry flavor. The ability to impact change is the prevailing reason participants say they are in the BzzAgent network, Chernov said, adding that participants also join to learn about products before they hit the mainstream. Money is not a factor, since BzzAgent has never paid its participants/bees.

At the time of the Al Fresco campaign, BzzAgent did not require its bees to disclose that they were affiliated with the marketing firm. Chernov told me that this was the prevailing model in the early years of word-of-mouth marketing. In 2005, BzzAgent changed its disclosure policy, and continues to require and enforce disclosure among its participants.

Since disclosure is part of the process, and bees are free to share negative information about a product if they find problems with it, Chernov told me that BzzAgent's version of word of mouth is an empowering new avenue for consumers. "Since the advent of advertising, marketers have chased consumers around a table. What word of mouth does is, it allows the consumer to stop and the advertiser to run right into them. The consumer is no longer the pursued. The consumer is the pursuer."

Word-of-mouth firm Zocalo told me it also requires disclosure. At the time this book went to press, Procter & Gamble's word-of-mouth firm, Tremor, was still not requiring disclosure from its participants. However, research is suggesting that disclosure can only help a word-of-mouth campaign. In 2006, BzzAgent partnered with researchers at Northeastern University to determine if disclosure has any practical benefits to the word-of-mouth process. The study revealed that disclosure didn't negatively impact word-of-mouth conversations. In fact, the relay rate increased when disclosure took place—meaning, if a bee told another person about a product and disclosed that he/she was part of an organized word-of-mouth campaign, the person learning this information was more likely to spread the word about the product. The Word of Mouth Marketing Association's ethics code calls for word-of-mouth advocates to disclose their relationship with marketers, telling others about any relationship they might have with a marketer, and about any products or incentives they may have received.

Consumer advocate Gary Ruskin is understandably concerned about Tremor and other word-of-mouth firms that do not require disclosure. In 2005, his group, Commercial Alert, petitioned the Federal Trade Commission to require companies that deploy these kinds of marketers to disclose their relationship with the firm. "We asked the FTC to require the paid shills to be disclosed as shills," Ruskin said. Commercial Alert argued that the FTC requires disclosure from other forms of media, such as search engines, magazines, and television infomercials. "The FTC came back and said, 'We agree with your principle. Sponsored consumers should disclose that they are sponsored.' But they wouldn't issue guidelines for what companies may or may not do," Ruskin said.

Commercial Alert also asked the FTC to investigate the word-of-mouth industry, but the FTC declined. Ruskin doesn't understand why. "It's dishonest advertising. It's stealth. The rules by which our society has operated for eighty years have largely been that advertising should be disclosed," he said. I asked Ruskin how widespread stealth marketing is. He told me that, due to its nature, there is no way to be sure. "They don't call it stealth marketing for nothing."

Word-of-mouth programs are not just in the cities, targeting urban hipsters like Camille. Moms across the country are also a target. According to Kevin Burke from Lucid Marketing, studies show that mothers are more likely than other consumers to tell a friend about a product or service they enjoyed, and more likely to trust another mom's recommendation over anyone else's.

Procter & Gamble [P&G] has used this to its advantage, launching a separate word-of-mouth program called Vocalpoint, which began as an extension of Tremor. As of May 2006, more than six-hundred-thousand moms across the country had joined the program. These women serve as personal endorsers for P&G products, as well as for the products of other companies that pay Vocalpoint to promote their brands. Each month, P&G sends moms product samples and gives them coupons and discounts. In return, the moms spread the word.[7] P&G has specifically sought out moms who make contact with many women each day. Statistically, these chatty Kathys speak to between twenty-five and thirty women per day, while the average mom speaks to five.

Vocalpoint's CEO Steve Knox—who also heads up Tremor—reiterated the importance of word of mouth in an interview with *Business-Week* in May 2006. He said, "We know that the most powerful form of marketing is an advocacy message from a trusted friend."[8]

I wanted to talk to Knox personally to learn more, but the company denied my request for an interview, referring me to other articles written about the program. Knox told *BusinessWeek* that when P&G is promoting a product through Vocalpoint, the advertising message differs from what is seen in commercials and print ads. That's because Vocalpoint wants its moms to be able to naturally start a conversation about the products they are promoting. For example, in a campaign for Dawn Direct Foam, commercials highlighted the product's grease-cutting power. Vocalpoint moms, on the other hand, received samples of the detergent, along with a pamphlet that explained why children would enjoy helping with the dishes because of the product's foamy consistency. Knox said, "We have to enable a conversation to take place," explaining that the company is aware that today's moms are talking about how kids are not doing enough chores around the house.

Paul Rand, from Zocalo Group, believes word-of-mouth marketing is entering its 2.0 stage and will reinvent itself in the future, reaching more people, beyond youth and urbanites. Moms are just the beginning of the expansion. As the field has evolved, some professionals, including Rand, have realized the limitations of reaching only the bees. "What has become increasingly known is, if something becomes hot, it can only cool down," he said, "And people who are attracted to shiny quarters very quickly move on to other shiny quarters."

To go beyond the bees and sustain a brand or product's word of mouth, Zocalo Group has developed a sophisticated method that targets other groups of consumers. Rand has identified five primary groups of influencers who, when made aware of a brand or product, naturally spread information about it. This results in numerous chains of buzz in the marketplace, which feed upon one another and extend word of mouth in terms of both time and reach. The first group of influencers are called Customer Evangelists; these are people who feel positively passionate about specific brands and eagerly spread the word to people they come into contact with. The second group of influencers are called Industry Eminents, who serve as leading voices in a particular area of expertise or industry. These are usually bloggers or members of the media who inform the public and share their opinions, which are valued by their audiences. The third group is Peer Influencers, who naturally enjoy telling others what brands and products they like, and have an impact on their friends' buying decisions. Zocalo believes that 10 percent of the population is naturally inclined to be Peer Influencers. The fourth group consists of the Bees, who are only interested in the hottest, newest products and tell others about those products, but lose interest and move on to newer products quickly. The fifth and final group is the Determined Detractors, who purposely spread negative word of mouth about products and brands.

Zocalo targets Evangelists, Eminents, Peer Influencers, Bees, and Detractors differently, because each group of influencers has differing motivations and sensibilities when it comes to spreading word of mouth. Rand wouldn't spare any examples to illustrate practical ways these five groups have been targeted to sustain word of mouth for a client. However, Zocalo's overall philosophy is that once these five groups of influencers are made aware of a brand or product and have viable opportunities to talk about it in their daily lives, consumers in the mainstream will encounter that brand or product numerous times. This experience will ingrain the brand or product in the minds of consumers, convincing them of that brand or product's worth, and will hopefully spark another wave of influencers, who will pass the word along further. Zocalo calls this method "continuous proving."

While WOMMA and many individual word-of-mouth firms like Zocalo stress that disclosure is necessary in word-of-mouth marketing practices, there is no surefire way to patrol word-of-mouth agents and ensure that they are disclosing their marketing relationships. Consumer advocate Ruskin has deeper concerns about how this type of marketing will impact the fabric of the culture. "The biggest problem—and it's a social problem on the grand scale—is that it encourages teenagers and others to treat their family and friends like pawns suitable for exploitation and manipulation," he said. "This is going to erode social trust. People are going to trust their family and friends less because they will wonder, 'Well, are they saying it because they think it, or because they are buzz marketers?' That fraying of social trust is a really serious matter. It's sad and suffocating if we are surrounded by corporate shills, especially if they are our family and friends."

It used to be that you could disconnect from advertising by simply turning off the television or closing a magazine. Now it hits us in waves as we go about our day, in the mail, on email, through text messages on cell phones, and through logos on the T-shirts of the people we pass. We have gotten very adept at ignoring these advances, but advertisers aren't going to let us get away that easily. Now marketing messages come through friends and acquaintances who are rewarded for slipping brand names into casual conversation. If only we had pop-up blockers in real life.

On one hand, I have to give kudos to the marketers who are finding ways to cut through the clutter. They have a job to do, a job that in this decade is more difficult than ever. Ten years ago, word of mouth was seen as grassroots and small-time, but in today's landscape, it's an essential part of any marketing strategy, so valued that corporations like Procter & Gamble are using it.

Still, marketers caused their own problem. And I can't deny that Gary Ruskin has a right to be concerned that our delicate and fraying social fabric could be irreparably damaged if word-of-mouth marketing hits a slippery slope. The government has given the business world increased speech protection over the past few decades, which has allowed ad creep to slither into so many parts of our lives. Covert word-of-mouth marketing is the newest tentacle on the beast. More regulations on word-of-mouth practices and other forms of ad creep could tame the beast, though it appears that the FTC is not at all interested in patrolling the industry. If marketers don't enforce ethical guidelines within the industry, ad creep and covert word-of-mouth practices will continue to snowball, leaving companies with an even more disillusioned, skeptical audience—and a great deal of fence mending to do.

CHAPTER 9

The Fence Mender

The fence mender has something to prove. He's making up for past mistakes in hopes of winning his way back to his woman's heart. He wants to repair his bad reputation, though no one is sure he can be trusted.

In today's advertising landscape, corporate America and Madison Avenue have many fences to mend to restore their images with women. Companies realize that in the past decade, many consumers have developed animosity toward big business due to ad bombardment, corporate scandals, overall sneakiness, and distaste for mega-conglomerates as a whole. A 2006 Gallup Poll revealed that advertising practitioners ranked only above car salesmen in a survey about ethics in professions. Only 11 percent of people believed that advertising practitioners have high ethical standards. Thirty-five percent said advertisers have low or very low ethical standards.[1]

When I asked thirty-two-year-old Miranda why she distrusted

corporations, she said, "It's the manipulation that I've seen more and more of. I realize that there is so much more that I'm not conscious of. I feel like some of the ethics have gone out of business. It's just become a huge money making factory. . . . It's just the widespread taking over of corporate America, and we're losing options. I feel like I'm a slave to this single entity that is controlling our media, our government. They are all in bed together in really complex ways. And I don't think I'm a conspiracy theorist."

Carol Cone, chairman and founder of Cone, Inc.—the nation's leading firm specializing in linking companies and causes—explained that the web has made companies more transparent, which has revealed the dark side of corporate America. "The Internet gave every consumer a major megaphone to say good or bad things about a company: where they buy their products, how they treat their employees, what they stand for. All of that you can find out. So the question is, do you feel better about them?" she told me.

Twentysomething Katie, from Oregon, answered that question when she told me, "I don't trust corporations. When I'm watching ads, I'm typically thinking, *What are they telling me that is not true, and what are they spinning to make it look better?"* Katie is aware that she can use the web to search for information about companies. She can find out which conglomerates own which brands, whether those brand's products are made by children in China, and whether their manufacturing practices are polluting the environment.

The marketing world is aware that the Internet is playing a crucial role in shaping consumer opinion. In a 2007 marketing convention, Steve Hayden, vice chairman of Ogilvy & Mather, said that bloggers are playing an active and growing role in shaping marketing campaigns. He said, "The blogosphere keeps us authentic, open, and honest—or it kills us."[2]

In addition to socially irresponsible business practices and corporate scandals like Enron and WorldCom, women are frustrated with companies slipping marketing messages into every facet of their lives. In addition to covert word-of-mouth marketing and product placement, more outrageous tactics are being tested. For example, the Kroger grocery chain tacked ads to the conveyor belts of its checkout aisles.[3] To promote its series *Rome,* HBO arranged for selected restaurants to give patrons complimentary bottles of cabernet sauvignon emblazoned with *Rome* labels.[4] I even remember reading a story about CBS printing its logo on eggs sold at the grocery store—not on the cartons, but on the individual eggs inside. Legendary American landmarks, museums, and ballparks are also being corporatized. Candlestick Park is now called Monster Park, named after the company that sponsors the stadium, Monster Cable Products Inc. The Smithsonian named the transportation section of its National Museum of American History after its corporate sponsor. It is called the General Motors Hall of Transportation. The directors of the Golden Gate Bridge are even entertaining ideas to encourage corporate sponsors to pay off a large deficit held by the bridge, in exchange for some kind of name recognition.[5] Airline passengers have even become captive audiences for sales presentations during flights. Ads are plastered to tray tables, and flight attendants read lengthy speeches on the overhead speaker, encouraging passengers to sign up for credit cards. On a recent flight, a passenger seated in front of me asked the flight attendant if she was required to sell the credit card. She nodded, looking a bit embarrassed, and said, "It's the only way we can make up for our cutbacks."

Lynn Upshaw, who wrote the book *Truth: New Rules for Marketing in a Skeptical World,* believes consumer skepticism is one of the major problems marketers are facing today. He cited a study that revealed that 75 percent of consumers would prefer to buy from a company that operates ethically, even if that means the products are more expensive. In another study, business professionals said that poor ethics have led to a lack of trust among consumers, which has a highly damaging effect on consumer behavior. At the same time, however, a 2006 study by the International Association of Business Communicators found that only 46 percent of respondents said that discussion about ethical and unethical behavior is encouraged in their organization.

Upshaw believes if the business world continues to avoid ethics, it will affect companies' bottom lines, because consumers are so fed up with unethical corporations and misleading marketing. Upshaw pointed to countless ethical lapses that have been reported in the media, including reports of undercover word-of-mouth firms that don't require disclosure, the pharmaceutical industry being fined by the government for misleading ads, and the Blockbuster video-rental chain settling claims with angry consumers after the company advertised no late fees but charged consumers for movies that weren't returned promptly.

He wrote in *Advertising Age,* "In too many marketing departments, integrity is essentially a backdrop to daily work rather than a prerequisite, an admirable trait that sits framed on a plaque instead of a necessary skill set that is integrated into marketing plans." Upshaw also wrote that companies that exercise integrity will gain more competitive advantage in the marketplace.[6]

Twenty-seven-year-old Cambria, from Austin, Texas, thinks ad bombardment has gotten out of control, particularly with product placement. "It drives me crazy. I was watching [the reality show] *Top Chef,* and it's like, 'Here is our Kenmore kitchen.' It's constant. And then they say, 'We will be going from our Kenmore kitchen to our site in our RAV4 SUV.' It bugs me," she said. "Then you get ad pop-ups on MySpace and ad pop-ups on AOL. Ads are everywhere, and I'm tired of it." Most of the women I spoke with echoed Cambria, saying they often feel bombarded by advertising as they go through their everyday lives.

Thirtysomething Vivian told me she can't completely escape online ads and spam. Still, she has her ways. "Everyone has two email addresses, one for spam and one for personal emails. Only your friends and family have the good email address. And the spam email address is for buying stuff, and you check that mailbox once a month," Vivian said. "You know, you have to play these games with the advertisers. It's dodgeball. I know I can't beat them, so I have to lead them to a different direction that won't be as invasive to my life."

Debbie, fifty-three, told me that ads are getting more obnoxious in order to demand her attention. The ad she couldn't escape was for Head On headache balm, a commercial that put the product on the map because it loudly and monotonously repeats the same phrase over and over again. "It was that annoying 'Head On, apply directly to the forehead. Head On, apply directly to the forehead. Head On.' Every time I saw that commercial, I had to change the channel. But I guess it worked, because I still remember it," she said. Many women I spoke to complained about the Head On commercial, though, like Debbie, all of them remembered the name of the product. Comparatively, they couldn't remember many of the other brands in the ads they liked or hated. The vice president of sales for Head On told one reporter that the company used focus groups to test several different advertising approaches, and found that the repetitive approach caused focus groups to remember the product much better than any other approach.[7] That brand recognition made it worth the risk of annoying some consumers. In 2005 and 2006, Head On reportedly sold more than five million units of the headache balm. Sales for Head On reached $6.5 million in 2006, up from just $1.9 million in 2005, according to Information Resources, Inc., which collects sales data from many national retailers. Head On's sales numbers are likely to be even higher, since Wal-Mart does not provide sales info to Information Resources, Inc.[8]

Nonetheless, consumers are irritated. A 2004 study from marketing consulting firm Yankelovich Partners found that 60 percent of consumers have a more negative opinion of marketing and advertising now than they did a few years prior. Sixty-one percent of respondents said they felt marketing and advertising were "out of control." Sixty-five percent said they constantly felt bombarded with too much marketing and advertising. The same percentage said there should be more legal regulations on marketing and advertising.[9] J. Walker Smith, president of Yankelovich, cited these statistics in a speech he gave at the annual American Association of Advertising Agencies conference in 2004. He told industry attendees that consumers were drowning in an overabundance of data and information that fails to meet their needs and desires. He said marketers should move away from the model of marketing saturation, clutter, and intrusiveness. While most marketers believe that spammers and telemarketers are the problem, Smith said the Yankelovich study showed that consumers are disenchanted with mainstream marketers as well.[10] "It's time for marketers to focus their business models on how to better deliver the kind of marketing that consumers really want, instead of assuming that consumers are happy fending off a daily deluge of marketing."

Marketing professionals have tried to improve their image using their own tried-and-true techniques. In 2006, the American Association of Advertising Agencies, the industry's largest trade group, hired a public relations firm to direct a public-image campaign on behalf of the industry.[11] According to *Advertising Age,* which reported details of the campaign, the firm GolinHarris was hired to "stave off negative headlines and burnish the industry's reputation with reporters and other influencers."

No PR campaign is going to change the way consumers feel about marketing professionals. And besides, the companies that hire the marketers are the ones that need to worry most about winning back the hearts of consumers. One of the most powerful ways they are doing that is through partnerships with charitable causes. A 2004 survey by the marketing firm Cone, Inc., found that 91 percent of consumers had a more positive image of a company or product when it supported a cause. Ninety percent said they would consider switching to another company if it was aligned with a cause.[12]

Companies are aware of this tendency and have rushed to connect their brands to charities, promoting their good deeds through advertising. This practice is widely known in the industry as "cause marketing." Carol Cone was one of the first marketing professionals to connect a company to an altruistic mission. Back in the 1980s, her company helped the Rockport Shoe Company market its shoes by raising awareness for better health through fitness walking. Back in those days, there was no such thing as cause marketing. It was just an idea Cone came up with. Fitness walking propelled Rockport to huge financial success. Since then, Cone has watched more and more companies implement cause-based campaigns. The reason is simple: "I always say that women, who control 80 to 85 percent of purchases, are relational. Women don't just want features and benefits. Women are about relationships, the relations that we have with our families, friends, and even companies today," Cone said. A woman is more likely to form a relationship with a company if it shares her concerns and uses its financial power to be socially responsible.

In 2007, companies were expected to spend nearly $1.5 billion on cause marketing projects, a growth of 23 percent since 2005, according to a study by the research firm IEG.[13] The causes of corporations vary. For example, Dawn dish soap devotes resources to saving birds and sea life hurt by pollution. Buick/Pontiac/GMC partnered with the organization A Million Thanks, which sends thank-you letters to American military troops. Whirlpool donates appliances to all Habitat for Humanity homes. In these three instances, the companies have made consumers aware of their charitable work through national advertising.

Many companies are tying their products and services to environmental causes, presumably because consumers are becoming increasingly concerned about global warming. Gallup conducts an annual environmental poll, which in 2007 found that surveyed Americans ranked the environment as the most important problem facing the country in the future. This awareness of the environment has led to numerous advertising and public relations firms' being dedicated to promoting green living, products, and awareness. General Electric has produced many commercials promoting its Ecomagination mission to solve environmental challenges. British Petroleum, also known as BP, created ads in 2002 heralding the company's investments in solar power, an effort to go beyond petroleum.[14]

When attempting to reach women through a cause-driven marketing effort, an enormous number of companies have chosen to partner with breast cancer awareness, research, and prevention causes, because many believe that breast cancer is the issue that female consumers care about most. Over the past ten years, a slew of corporations has made donations to breast cancer causes and have advertised those donations in the marketplace. The drill goes a little something like this: The company creates a pink version of one of its products. The company advertises that it will donate a portion of its proceeds from the sales of that product to a breast cancer charity. The company then benefits from that contribution in two ways. First, the company creates positive PR with its customer base by appearing to be an ethical, caring company. Second, the company brings in more sales because so many consumers are moved to purchase the pink product. The amount donated by the company is usually not significant enough to hurt its profits, especially since it's selling more units of the pink item. Some might call this a win-win. Others would ask why the company isn't donating more in the name of charity. It's tough to condemn any person or company for donating to a cause, but when a multimillion-dollar company is benefiting more than it is giving, there is obvious room for criticism.

After being diagnosed with breast cancer, author Barbara Ehrenreich wrote about the corporatization of breast cancer in a 2001 *Harper's* magazine first-person story called "Welcome to Cancerland: A Mammogram Leads to a Cult of Pink Kitsch." In it, she wrote, "Now breast cancer has blossomed from wallflower to the most popular girl at the corporate charity prom. While AIDS goes begging and low-rent diseases like tuberculosis have no friends at all, breast cancer has been able to count on Revlon, Avon, Ford, Tiffany, Pier 1, Estée Lauder, Ralph Lauren, Lee Jeans, Saks Fifth Avenue, JCPenney, Boston Market, Wilson athletic gear—and I apologize to those I've omitted."[15]

Campbell's is another example. In 2006, the soupmaker sparked criticism for its breast cancer contribution during October, which is Breast Cancer Awareness Month. Campbell's partnered with the Kroger grocery chain, replacing its legendary red-and-white soup labels with pink labels, and donated $250,000 to the Susan G. Komen Foundation. Campbell's benefited from strong sales because the Kroger grocery chain bought seven million cans of Campbell's soup—twice as many as it normally buys in October. Kroger believed the breast cancer cause would bring in stronger sales.[16]

Women's marketing expert and writer Holly Buchanan wrote about the Campbell's campaign on her marketing blog. "I love the fact that Campbell's Soup, which is a very 'mom-friendly' product, aligns themselves with Breast Cancer awareness. I think it is a good fit with their brand and product image," she wrote. But Buchanan went on to note the obvious shortcomings. "Campbell's will donate $250,000 to the Susan G. Komen Foundation through Kroger. Now, that is a very large contribution—nothing to sneeze at. But here's where there's a little disconnect. . . . That works out to about 3.5 cents per can. Now—if I do the math, that means if I really splurge and buy—say—10 cans of soup, I'm feeling really good because my purchase will result in . . . 35 cents going to breast cancer awareness and research. Hmmm . . . wait a minute . . . 35 cents?? Don't get me wrong—I applaud Campbell's efforts to support a cause that is very important to their customers. But I just wonder . . . if a can of soup costs, let's say, around $1.89—any way they could up the amount donated per can?"[17]

Visitors to Buchanan's blog posted their own comments, many of which echoed her views. One visitor, named Tish, wrote, "Cause marketing for breast cancer sounds great. Terrific visual impact for Campbell's. But you're right—$0.35 is just not much money. Face it, the company is doing this simply to get attention to its brand. Otherwise, it could much more easily donate the $250,000 from the corporate contributions budget and put out a press release about its good deed. Either way, I'm sure Campbell's gets the tax deduction."

John Faulkner, director of brand communications for Campbell Soup Company, responded to the criticism, telling me that Campbell's believes its $250,000 contribution was a meaningful donation. Campbell's joined in the partnership after being asked by Kroger. In the past, Campbell's had been more aligned with heart-health causes, because it produces low-sodium soups that are better for blood pressure and heart health. Campbell's decided to partner with Kroger and make a contribution to breast cancer research because the company believes that the cause is especially relevant to its primary consumers—women who do the household grocery shopping. Campbell's wanted to show women that the company was aligned with their interests. "We're proud of what we did, and we think our brand is special—an icon brand with an opportunity to align with a special cause," Faulkner said. "The critics can be critics, but [the cause] wouldn't be big if companies like Campbell's and others weren't participating and helping to drive awareness," he said.

Faulkner believes that Campbell's participation brought more awareness to the cause because the iconic soup label is so recognizable and the soup is in so many of America's homes. He also pointed out that many pink products that companies create to raise awareness are expensive, meaning that in order for consumers to participate, they must spend at least $50. The pink Campbell's cans made it possible for many more people to participate, because the soup costs less than $1, Faulkner said.

He added that criticism is warranted at companies that spend more money promoting their donation than they spend on the actual donation. This, he said, was not the case with Campbell's. The company spent about $40,000 promoting the pink-can initiative. Faulkner said Campbell's intends to participate in breast cancer awareness as well as heart-related causes in future years.

When I asked Buchanan about her blog entry, she said, "Consumers today are more skeptical about cause marketing. They want to feel companies are genuine and authentic in their efforts to support worthy causes. Too many companies use cause marketing purely as a way to get PR and sell more stuff." Buchanan echoed Cone, telling me that the web has increased transparency, making it easy for consumers to find out whether their cause-marketing attempts are less than genuine. "If a company makes a million dollars in profit off a cause-marketing campaign and gives the cause $250,000—will consumers really feel good about that?"

Buchanan asked. "If your goal is to make money, this model makes sense from a pure bottom line point of view. But if the goal is to build brand loyalty, to make your customers feel good about buying your product, this model can backfire on you."

The San Francisco–based nonprofit Breast Cancer Action has tapped into this issue with its project Think Before You Pink. The project educates consumers about the widespread cause-marketing efforts tied to breast cancer, and how to determine which companies are giving adequate charitable contributions. "It's very clear to me that breast cancer is the poster child of cause marketing," said Barbara Brenner, the executive director of Breast Cancer Action. Brenner is a two-time breast cancer survivor who wrote an op-ed about this issue back in 2000. Her article incited widespread response from breast cancer survivors and consumers. That feedback led the organization to launch the Think Before You Pink project.

Brenner said breast cancer research is a popular corporate cause because women have an obvious concern about breast cancer. Companies have found that sticking a pink ribbon on their products helps them stand out in the competitive marketplace. And although the Susan G. Komen Foundation has been assertive and successful in bringing companies to the cause, Breast Cancer Action is critical of the foundation because, Brenner said, it doesn't have strict requirements for partnering companies. Brenner's final point about the popularity of breast cancer as a corporate cause came as a surprise. "It's talking about sex without talking about sex. If you can say the word 'breast' without getting slammed, it's titillating." Brenner isn't the first person to make this association. Samantha King, author of the book *Pink Ribbons, Inc.: Breast Cancer and the Politics of Philanthropy*, once told a reporter, "The breast is associated with motherhood and nurturance and also sex. Those are things that hold a lot of appeal and are highly valued in our culture."[18]

Think Before You Pink asks consumers to look at packaging closely before buying a product that benefits breast cancer. Consumers should look to see if the packaging includes specific information about the donation and the benefiting organization.

"Can you tell how much of the purchase price goes to the cause? Can you figure out what it is supporting? What kind of research?" she asked, adding that many companies put a cap on their total donation, regardless of the number of units sold, and that the packaging should disclose this as well. Think Before You Pink encourages women to write to companies and ask them these questions. The organization's website includes steps for creating an inquiry letter. Brenner said women should also ask companies how much they spent to market their pink-ribbon product, and what the company is doing to ensure that its products aren't contributing to the cancer epidemic. For example, many dairy products contain Bovine Growth Hormone, which might be a cancer causer, according to some studies. Numerous cosmetic products contain toxins and carcinogens. Breast Cancer Action challenges companies by asking them these questions, but companies often do not respond, Brenner said.

Breast Cancer Action requires any companies that wish to partner with them to answer these same questions. Not surprisingly, Breast Cancer Action doesn't have many corporate sponsors. "In August [in preparation for Breast Cancer Awareness Month], we'll hear from a PR firm who has a corporate client who is interested in getting into the cause marketing. . . . And we'll say, 'Maybe. Can you answer these questions?' And then we'll never hear from them again," she said. Brenner added that some breast cancer organizations would like to challenge their partnering corporations with these questions; however, they don't proceed because they don't want to lose their corporate funding.

In the world of cause marketing, there is a label for halfhearted campaigns: Cause Lite, Cone said. "It's companies utilizing it for public relations. They donate $250,000 to some not-for-profit and they spend $2 million telling people about it," she said. "It's not best practice." And while some of Cause Lite will skate by, Cone believes that it will be obvious to many consumers. Instead, companies should commit to an all-encompassing strategy, which blends cause marketing with corporate responsibility. Cone referred to corporate responsibility as "the whole ball of wax," meaning that the company publicly reports and implements forward-thinking approaches in its operations, its governance practices, and its giving, environmental, and employee policies. Social responsibility should be embedded in the company—or, as Cone said, "part of the company's DNA."

While older consumers appreciate socially responsible companies, Generation Y expects them. "They are prosocial and empowered to change the world. They are demanding it as employees, consumers, and citizens. Companies are just beginning to get it," Cone said, adding, "You can't market to young people and have your shoes made in a sweatshop. Nike learned that the hard way, and then they got religion."

Demographers describe Generation Y as a more socially responsible subset of the population. Statistics show that teens and twentysomethings have one of the highest percentages of volunteerism in decades, in part because many high schools require students to complete a specified number of volunteer hours. Their lifelong exposure to the web has also given these young consumers more information about the world and the image of the United States in the international community. Generation Y also cares greatly about the environment—which is not surprising, since these consumers will likely see some of the major ramifications of global warming and pollution in their own lifetimes. In a 2006 Harris Poll, college students aged 18 to 30 ranked a company's social responsibility as more important than a brand's image or a celebrity endorsement.[19] Generational expert Claire Raines told me that this resurgence in social concern can also be attributed to Generation Y's exposure to some of the world's most horrific events in recent memory, namely 9/11, Hurricane Katrina, and the deadly tsunami in Thailand. Their exposure to these human tragedies at a younger, more impressionable age has had a significant impact on their personal development.

Marketing consultant Lisa Johnson, who wrote *Mind Your Xs and Ys,* a book about marketing to the younger generations, said it is no surprise that Gen Y college students are studying abroad in record numbers. "What it does is, it incites a desire that the world is bigger than myself, and I want to make a difference and respect the needs of other people. It's a give-back spirit that is unparalleled. They consider what they buy to be like a vote. They do more hands-on give-back. They are reinventing volunteerism."

Companies also realize young people's networking power through online social communities like MySpace and Facebook. "This generation is full of sharp watchdogs. We're in a new environment where we can spread something around in about a day. Because if I have five hundred friends in my online network, and all of our friends have five hundred friends, things spread very quickly," Johnson said. For example, the website ExxposeExxon.com was started by a coalition of environmental awareness groups to educate the public about its viewpoint on the oil company. One of the tools on the website is the Tell A Friend link, which allows visitors to send information instantaneously to multiple email addresses. This way, they can easily alert many friends and family members to the cause.

Consumers are communicating about products and companies through chain emails, website comments, and videos on YouTube. Johnson pointed to a website posting written a couple of years ago, where one person complained about a faulty bike lock manufactured by the Kryptonite lock company. To illustrate this defect, the person used a Bic pen to easily pop open the lock. The posting spread like wildfire, forcing the company to release a replacement lock. "This is a generation that cares about treating people right and doing things the right way. This is a generation that has embraced social justice, and they are looking at the world in a new way," Johnson said.

Indeed, many of the young women I spoke to were looking for socially responsible companies. Twentysomething Katie said she would much rather buy from a company that is doing the right thing for the environment and its workers, even if the company's commercial is not that interesting. "I don't need my ad campaigns to be the sexy guy at the bar hitting on me. I want something to be behind it, more solid information that I can have proven to me somehow."

I asked consumer advocate Gary Ruskin why young people are particularly moved by cause marketing. "The younger generation is very idealistic, and so there is this tremendous dissonance between the idealism of this generation and the cynicism of America's large companies. So corporate America has to crack that problem every hour." I asked Ruskin if he would compare companies that bombard women with ad creep and clutter to pushy, rebellious guys—or worse, stalkers. Cause marketing, in that sense, is the stalker's way of showing up on the doorstep with a bouquet of flowers. Ruskin was intrigued by my metaphor and agreed wholeheartedly. "Why does the sentimental stalker exist?" he asked rhetorically. "The cumulative effect is billions and billions of dollars. Marketers know what works. The sentimental pitch works, and for a lot of companies, it's all they have left. They can't say, 'We're honorable.' They can't say, 'Our product is good.' All they can say is, 'We'll throw a couple of quarters in the direction of a good nonprofit.' And that's all they've got."

Gen Yer Cambria, a twentysomething and from Austin, has been involved in various conservation and environmental causes since she was a child, and she buys from companies that partner with charities. She is currently wearing a bracelet that she purchased through the Red campaign. Proceeds from Red products go to the Global Fund, which provides AIDS drugs to people in Africa. Cambria bought her Red bracelet at the Gap, one of Red's corporate partners. "I saw it at the store when I was there, and I just read the information. And then I saw it on *Oprah*," Cambria said, referring to an episode of Oprah's show that featured the U2 singer Bono, who implored viewers to buy Red products at the Gap, Armani, and other retailers. "I really like Bono. This is something that he started, and he gets involved in really great causes."

But Red has some critics. Ben Davis, creator of a website called Buylesscrap.org, is one of them. His site asks consumers to give directly to the Global Fund, instead of through branded philanthropic partnerships like Red. He told *Advertising Age,* "Shopping is not a solution. Buy less. Give more." In that same article, *Advertising Age* estimated that Red's corporate retailers have raised $25 million for the Global Fund, but have spent $100 million on marketing the campaign, which has prompted criticism from watchdog groups. In response, Red's cochair Bobby Shriver issued a statement saying that *Advertising Age's* $100 million estimate was off by more than 50 percent. He wrote, "Any company worth its weight in salt knows it doesn't exist to give away money. Red gives our partners a way to do good and turn a profit doing so."

Trent Stamp, president of Charity Navigator, a nonprofit watchdog group, took an evenhanded approach, telling *Advertising Age,* "The Red campaign can be a good start or it can be a colossal waste of money, and it all depends on whether this edgy, innovative campaign inspires young people to be better citizens or just gives them an excuse to feel good about themselves while they buy an overpriced item they don't really need."[20]

Cambria told me that she probably wouldn't have purchased the Red bracelet if not for the cause that was tied to it. "If a certain amount of proceeds go to a specific organization, I have a tendency to buy that product," she said. Cambria explained that she would like to donate more money to her favorite causes, but, she currently needs nearly all of her income to make ends meet. However, if she needs to buy a product, and the brand is making a contribution to a cause, she will choose that product over a competing brand, even if it means paying a few extra dollars. That way, she can make a charitable contribution and buy what she needs. "It's like killing two birds with one stone," she told me.

That is why Red makes sense. If partnerships like Red are the only way to motivate companies to do the right thing, and consumers can't be motivated to give as much as they buy, these philanthropical partnerships are the best meeting point. If consumers grow more suspicious of these kinds of partnerships, the marketplace will probably see less of them.

But beyond charitable giving, companies could mend some fences in more subtle ways, Lisa Johnson told me. Women appreciate companies that perform great customer service, pay attention to the details, and make the shopping experience a pleasurable one. "What [a woman] loves are smaller gestures," Johnson said. "It's the little things. She really notices the details, the way you are showing up, doing small, helpful, problem-solving things. That is better than one grand Super Bowl ad." Johnson explained that Apple has done a great job at addressing the little things. "When you go to buy your iPod, it's so fun to unpack that thing. It's effortlessly simple. . . . It's great to be in the store. It feels so good, it makes you want to exhale. They bring in a person called a 'genius' to teach classes in the store for free, because they know that people want to learn from other people." Johnson said the company is equally good at doing the big things the right way. "Their computers are already loaded with interesting software. Their computers back up data automatically. I can go on and on with all of the big and small ways they have moved me. They let go of old [products]. They teach. The online tutorials are brilliant. I love their humor. They use music."

Most of all, Johnson said, Apple pays attention to the needs and desires of younger people, whom she calls the Connected Generation. "When file sharing became a problem with Napster, everybody else either went bankrupt or started suing. Apple came up with a solution. At that point, the iPod and iTunes didn't exist. They created the software, the store, and the product. It's a complete solution. They work seamlessly together. They joined with the Connected Generation and wanted to do it. They are smarties."

We are in an era of consumer control and transparency. Consumers know from the Fortune 500 list that corporations net billions of dollars each year, and CEOs take home millions. The gap between rich and poor has only grown over the past decade, and consumers view fat-cat corporations as part of the problem. This has forced companies to go on the defense to secure their reputations. But fence mending is not an overnight solution. It requires a long-term commitment. A random $250,000 check to a charity doesn't cut it. Female consumers are looking for problem solving, social responsibility, and meaningful charitable giving. They can easily spot disingenuous cause marketing and will stop at nothing to alert their fellow consumers to phonies. Smart companies aren't simply supporting breast cancer causes to follow the pack. They are linking to causes that make sense for their brands. For example, GE supports Autism Speaks, an organization cofounded by Vice Chairman Bob Wright, whose grandson has autism. Dawn dishwashing soap supports wildlife preservation, because Dawn is used to clean oil residue off of sea animals. Origins and Aveda cosmetics don't simply donate to environmental causes—their entire businesses are molded around environmental protection. In addition, companies are linking up with respected philanthropic figures, like Maya Angelou and Bono, to endorse their efforts.

These kinds of steps illustrate that we are in an era of consumer control, and that is good for women. A couple of decades ago, companies didn't have to support charities or adhere to socially responsible policies. Today it's required. That only goes to show that consumers are in the power position. The more aware and picky women become, the more they will force companies to produce better ads and better products, as well as to create better charitable partnerships.

Epilogue

In all of my interviews with women, my last question was the same: What should marketers be doing better? My question usually resulted in a few moments of silence, as these thoughtful, honest women pondered what they really wanted. But soon the answers flowed.

"I've started to buy your product, so entice me to buy more. Send me coupons. Don't let it be a one-time shot. Keep drawing me in," Andrea, thirty, told me. Los Angeles single woman Kysha, who is African American, told me that she would like to see more diversity in ads. "Everybody likes to see an image of themselves on television," she said. Tesia, who is also African American, told me when companies do try to reach African Americans, they "urbanize" their ads in stereotypical ways, "It's always, like, this sassy music going on. And there is a woman with an attitude. And there is always some hip-hop song that they've made up. It really annoys me," she said. "Like, the McDonald's commercials on BET are different [from ads on other channels]. It's always, like, 'Yo, if I'm hungry, I go to Mickey D's, you know what I'm saying?'" Tesia told me, mimicking the ads and laughing. "There is always some B- or C-list rap artist making up a rap about the Quarter Pounder." Tesia also believes that commercials like this contribute to stereotypes. "They draw conclusions that all black people must act this way, all Hispanic people must act this way, all Indian people must act this way. You know, all black people are into rap music, and it's all they can relate to," she said.

Vivian, who is Asian American, told me that while she isn't bothered when she sees an ad that doesn't feature Asians, she gets excited when she sees one that does. "Like, there's an ad right now that has an Asian family, and the mom is asking the daughter to help her convince the dad to get a new refrigerator. I was like, 'Oh my god, it's a whole Asian family.' Usually, if I see an Asian person in a commercial, it's one token girl. But this was a whole family."

It's not always an issue of minority versus white. Colleen, who is forty-four and Caucasian, said that Madison Avenue doesn't reflect the lives of people in middle America. She rarely sees an ad that reflects her life in Omaha, Nebraska. Instead, most ads she sees are set in metropolitan areas, with ultracool singles who look nothing like her. "I don't feel like they try to reach the commonness anymore. It's always trying to reach the extreme. Nobody wants to deal with the common, the middle, the plain Jane. Nobody wants that anymore, yet there are still a lot of us out there."

Thirtysomethings Laura and Kelly, two women from opposite coasts, suggested that ads get more intelligent. "Don't always aim for the middle ground—aim for the high end, and assume that people can catch up," Laura said. Kelly told me, "I wish advertisers would assume the intelligence of their audience, and then if [consumers] don't get it, they can think about it," she said.

Melanie, from the suburbs of Chattanooga, Tennessee, said, "Don't push so hard. Make a good product, keep the price reasonable, and don't change it just for the sake of change. Keep your ads informative, realistic, and not deliberately offensive." Fiftysomething Barbara, from Pittsburgh, echoed Melanie when she said, "Just keep it simple."

Twenty-seven-year-old Maria, from Miami, said, "Marketers need to find the right balance between reality and aspiration—we all want to be represented in the media, whether it be in a magazine ad or a TV commercial. But we also aspire to reach goals and live better lives. Some might suggest that advertising misguides people into believing that they aren't happy and that they need more, more, more. While that could certainly be true, when done the right way, advertising can actually inspire people to achieve what they yearn for."

Miranda said, "They should prove that they care about society. They should show me that they are a company and a humanitarian force as well. They should prove that they see their responsibility to their world by contributing to others in meaningful ways—that way I know, or at least feel like, they see beyond the profit. I want to trust a product and a company in that way. I'll always be skeptical, and I may not run out and buy a particular item even if I see their soft side, but I'm far more likely to go their direction when the need arises."

Certainly, there is no way an ad or company can please all women. I actually sympathize with the companies and ad firms responsible for trying to. But I think there are also universal truths marketers can rely on. Women want to be courted. They are looking for diversity. They want to be asked for their opinion. They want a gentle hand, an inspiring message, a humorous moment, a good deal, and a company that befriends them, sincerely attempting to produce an ad that they like.

When I began writing this book, my goal was to show female readers how companies are eager to reach them, and to amuse these women with the flirtation techniques companies use to meet their goals. It wasn't long before I realized that the information in my book could actually empower women to improve advertising.

Experts, authors, and marketing consultants who specialize in the women's market have helped to spark reform. Their insights are starting to convince Madison Avenue to rethink old ideologies about female consumers. But most are frustrated by how long it takes Madison Avenue to learn new tricks. To offer an example, one women's consultant told me that when she attended a large advertising conference last year, she sat in on a session on marketing to women and saw no sign of the top brass from any marketing firms or corporations. She wasn't surprised that the companies sent token low-level employees to represent them for "the women's session."

She and others cannot deny that when it comes to invoking change, the best business books and most brilliant lectures pale in comparison to the billions of dollars that the Patricias, Melanies, and Kyshas of the world are spending.

I know that effective ads can compel women to buy products. But few women boycott brands that produce ads that annoy or insult them. They aren't paying close enough attention, and few realize they could make a difference. When I asked women whether they had ever boycotted a brand because of advertising, very few said they had. The exception was Kansas City forty-five-year-old Kay, who told me, "I remember our family stopped going to Burger King after [seeing] commercials in the late 1980s that stated, 'Sometimes you gotta break the rules.' My husband and I were trying to raise our children to follow rules, and felt this commercial was not setting a good example."

I believe that women can use the information in this book to better analyze the messages they receive from advertising, and that they can take that information into the stores with them. That way, they will recognize which companies are aligned with their sensibilities and interests, and which are off the mark. In today's cluttered ad world, where we are bombarded by sales pitches at every turn, it's much easier to ignore ads than it is to pay close attention. But I hope, going forward, you will remember brands and marketing messages like you remember the characters and story lines on your favorite TV shows. I hope you will ignore the advances of companies that aren't working hard enough to win your heart. I hope you will communicate with companies through their websites, and that you will participate when someone calls to ask you to answer a few questions for "market research." Let your voice be heard.

We are living and shopping in an era when companies are ever vigilant about the effectiveness of their ads, and ever interested in communicating with their customers through the web. That's the way to see major change from Madison Avenue and corporate America. There is no way to completely escape the bombardment of advertising, but we women have the power to force the flirts of the ad world to step up their game.

Notes

CHAPTER 1 • The Scholar

1. Tom Neveril, "Behavior Defines Consumers," *Advertising Age,* 16 July 2007.

2. Jack Neff, "Steal This Bag . . . and Look Inside," *Advertising Age,* 7 May 2007.

3. Margot Hornblower, "Great Xpectations," *Time,* 9 June 1997.

4. Ibid.

5. Lillie Guyer, "Scion Connects in Out of Way Places," *Advertising Age,* 21 February 2005, 38.

6. Mary Brown and Carol Orsborn, PhD, *Boom: Marketing to the Ultimate Power Consumer, the Baby-Boomer Woman* (New York: Amacom, 2006), 126.

7. Ibid., 129.

8. Ibid.

9. Matt Kinsey, "The Latest Consumers You Need to Get to Know," *Advertising Age,* 23 July 2007.

CHAPTER 2 • The Best Friend

1. Theresa Howard, "Jetta crash ads come back for an encore," *USA Today,* 4 December 2006.

CHAPTER 3 • The Fan

1. Joseph Carroll, "Who's Worried about Their Weight?" Gallup Poll, 9 August 2005.

2. Theresa Howard, "Customers go for fresh-looking 7UP," *USA Today,* 9 September 2006.

3. Claudia H. Deutsch, "Not Getting Older, Just More Scrutinized," *The New York Times,* 11 October 2006.

4. "It's Official: Marketers Can't Afford Not to Build Relationships with Boomers," 26 March 2007, www.thirdage.com/about/press_room/subs/20070526_jwt_boomers.html.

5. Jack Neff, "Unilever Resuscitates the Demo Left for Dead," *Advertising Age,* 28 May 2007.

6. Abbey Klaassen, "Media Players Go after Free-Spending Boomers," *Advertising Age,* 3 September 2007.

7. Census Bureau Current Population Reports, "Children's Living Arrangements and Characteristics," March 2002, page 11, www.census.gov/prod/2003pubs/p20-547.pdf.

8. Alexandra Robbins, *The Overachievers* (New York: Hyperion, 2006), 14.

9. Kristin Rowe-Finkbeiner, *The F-Word* (Emeryville, CA: Seal Press, 2004), 1.

10. Noy Thrupkaew, "Daughters of the Revolution," *The American Prospect,* October 2003.

11. Theresa Howard, "Suave's message to moms connects," *USA Today,* 23 October 2006.

12. Paul Brent, "The Family Guy," *Marketing* magazine, 1 May 2006.

13. Ivy McClure Stewart and Kate Kennedy, "Madison Avenue Man: He's Dumb, He's a Slob, He's Selling Kleenex," *Women's Quarterly,* spring 2001.

CHAPTER 4 • The Player

1. Bob Garfield, "Bob Garfield's Chaos Scenario," *Advertising Age,* 13 April 2005.

2. Harris Poll, "Almost Three-Quarters of All U.S. Adults—An Estimated 163 Million—Go Online," 12 May 2005.

3. Pew Internet & American Life Project, "How Women and Men Use the Internet," 28 December 2005.

4. Nat Ives, "Where Have All the Girls Gone?," *Advertising Age,* 16 July 2007.

5. "TNS Media Intelligence Forecasts 1.7 Percent Increase in U.S. Advertising Spending for 2007," press release, 12 June, 2007, www.tns-mi.com/news/06122007.htm.

6. Abbey Klaassen, "Advertisers Can't Afford to Quit MySpace," *Advertising Age,* 30 July 2007.

7. Abbey Klaassen, "What's Making Friends with a MySpace User Worth?," *Advertising Age,* 23 April 2007.

8. Brian Morrissey, "Maybelline Takes a Page from MySpace," *Adweek,* 6 February 2006.

9. Stuart Elliot, "Advertisers Want Something Different," *The New York Times,* 23 May 2005.

10. Tricia Duryee, "Advertisers turn to small screen," *The Seattle Times,* 14 September 2006.

11. Nat Ives, "Interactive Viral Campaigns Ask Consumers to Spread the Word," *The New York Times,* 18 February 2005.

12. Pop Culture Junk Mail, 19 July 2005, http://pcjm.blogspot.com/2005/07/everybody-salsa.html.

13. Pew Internet & American Life Project, "Teens and Technology," 27 July 2005.

14. David Bauder, "Scared Advertisers," Associated Press, 22 March 2006.

15. Louise Story, "Assigning Ratings to Commercials Turns Out to Be a Tricky Task," *The New York Times,* 13 March 2007.

16. U.S. Census Bureau, "More Diversity, Slower Growth," March 18, 2004, www.census.gov/Press-Release/www/releases/archives/population/001720.html.

17. David Kiley, "Laughing Out Loud in Spanish," *BusinessWeek,* 16 March 2006.

18. Ibid.

19. U.S. Census Bureau, press release, 26 September 2000, www.census.gov/Press-Release/www/2000/cb00-158.html.

20. U.S. Census Bureau, press release, 30 August 2005, www.census.gov/Press-Release/www/releases/archives/income_wealth/005647.html.

21. Target Market News, "Buying Power of Black America," 12th edition, http://targetmarketnews.com/publications.htm.

22. Eugene Morris, "The Evolution of Targeting the Black Audience," AdvertisingAge.com, 11 September 2007, http://adage.com/bigtent/post?article_id=120380.

23. Valerie Lynn Gray, "Going after our dollars—Black consumers are the targets but corporate America may not be giving back to the community," *Black Enterprise,* July 1997.

24. Lisa Sanders, "'Black Enterprise' Magazine Chief Calls Ad Industry 'Racist,'" *Advertising Age,* 13 June 2006.

25. Stuart Elliot, "Procter & Gamble is giving a higher priority to developing campaigns aimed at black consumers," *The New York Times,* 13 June 2003, sec. C, p. 5.

26. PR Newswire, "Procter & Gamble Ignites National Conversation on Beauty Among African American Women," press release, 9 August, 2007.

27. Kellyanne Conway and Celinda Lake, *What Women Really Want* (New York: Free Press, 2005), 10.

28. Sam Roberts, "51% of Women Are Now Living Without a Spouse," *The New York Times,* 16 January 2007.

29. Business wire, "Car Rentals, Gym Memberships and iPods . . . Oh My!; National Gay Newspaaer Guild Unveils Above-Average Gay, Lesbian Consumers in Lesbian Consumers in Latest Installment of 20 Year Reader Poll," press release, 1 August 2005.

30. Commercialcloset.com, Subaru ad, "It's Not A Choice," www.commercial-closet.org/cgi-bin/iowa/portrayals.html?record=465.

31. Commercialcloset.com, IKEA ad, "Living Room," www.commercialcloset.org/cgi-bin/iowa/portrayals.html?record=2995.

32. Commercial Closet, American Express ad, www.commercialcloset.org/cgi-bin/iowa/portrayals.html?record=334.

33. Andrew Hampp, "An Ad in Which Boy Gets Girl . . . or Boy," *Advertising Age,* 6 August 2007.

34. Jean Kilbourne, *Can't Buy My Love* (New York: Simon & Schuster, 1999), 39.

CHAPTER 5 • The Show-off

1. "TNS Media Intelligence Forecasts 1.7 Percent Increase in U.S. Advertising Spending for 2007," press release, 12 June 2007, www.tns-mi.com/news/06122007.htm.

2. Ira Teinowitz, "A Funny Thing Happened on the Way to the White House," *Advertising Age,* 30 July 2007.

3. Faye Brookman, "Clairol Herbal Essences: Jane Owen," *Advertising Age,* 28 June 1999.

4. Ibid.

5. Laura Petrecca, "Those with giant ailments dance for big Pepto relief," *USA Today,* 19 March 2007.

6. Kamau High, "Pregnancy Test's Clearblue Odyssey," *Adweek,* 18 December 2006.

7. Jack Neff, "Clorox Finds Running with Lions Effective," *Advertising Age,* 13 March 2006.

8. Bob Garfield, "Haggar, Crispin flush decency down the toilet," *Advertising Age,* 4 December 2006.

9. Devin Leonard, "Viral Ads: It's an epidemic," *Fortune,* 2 October 2006.

10. Nat Ives, "Interactive viral campaigns ask consumers to spread the word," *The New York Times,* 18 February 2005.

11. Tim Arango, "Shaver Buzz Is Philips' Dream," *The New York Post,* 23 June 2006.

12. Stuart Elliot, "Critics to Marketers: Suicide Is No Joke," *The New York Times,* 14 March 2007.

13. Jack Neff, "Unilever, P&G battle hits YouTube," *Advertising Age,* 12 February 2007.

14. CTV.ca news staff, "YouTube bride video has hair company roots," 2 February 2007, www.ctv.ca/servlet/ArticleNews/story/CTVNews/20070201/You_tube_folo_070201.

15. Sam Roberts, "To Be Married Means to Be Outnumbered," *The New York Times,* 15 October 2006.

16. U.S. Census Bureau of Household and Family Statistics, 2000.

17. Tanya Irwin, "Kmart Diversifies Holiday Spots," *AdWeek,* 25 November 2002.

18. Seth Stevenson, "Verizon uses race to make you look," *Slate,* 26 April 2004.

19. Harris Poll, "Divorce seen as biggest challenge to stable American family life," 18 October 2006.

20. David Kiley, "Ford Affirms Gay Publication Support. No Victory for AFA," *Business Week,* 14 December 2005.

21. Andrew Adam Newman, "Pigs with Cellphones, but No Condoms," *The New York Times,* 18 June 2007.

22. Ira Teinowitz, "T-Mobile yanks ads in response to AFA criticism," *Advertising Age,* 24 July 2006.

23. Jack Neff, "Wildmon wins PR battles, but not his gay-ads war," *Advertising Age,* 12 December 2005.

24. Matthew Creamer, "Survey: Marketers Can't Grade Agencies but Fail Them Anyway," *Advertising Age,* 26 February 2007.

25. Gregory Solman and Andrew McMains, "Short-term parking for car CMOs," *Adweek,* 4 June 2007.

CHAPTER 6 • The Dreamboat

1. Indiana University, "Men Do Hear—But Differently Than Women, Brain Images Show," 28 November 2000.

2. Julie Bosman, "Stuck at the Edge of the Ad Game," *The New York Times,* 22 November 2005.

3. Ibid.

4. Ibid.

5. Eleftheria Parpis, "Does Gender Matter?," *Adweek,* 28 November 2005.

6. Ibid.

7. Ibid.

8. Ibid.

9. Jean Kilbourne, *Can't Buy My Love* (New York: Simon & Schuster, 1999), 28.

10. Jack Neff, "Don't let beauty get too real," *Advertising Age,* 16 April 2007.

11. Jack Neff, "Soft Soap," *Advertising Age,* 24 September 2007.

12. Theresa Howard, "Dove ads enlist all shapes, styles, sizes," *USA Today,* 28 August 2005.

CHAPTER 7 • The Romantic

1. Raksha Arora and Lydia Saad, "Marketing to the Mass Affluent," Gallup Poll, 9 December 2004.

CHAPTER 8 • The Sneak

1. Jenna Schnuer, "Brands Toil to Make Surfers Loyal," *Advertising Age,* 21 June 2004, S2.

2. Motoko Rich, "Product Placement Deals Make Leap From film to Books," *The New York Times,* 12 June 2006.

3. Aline van Duyn, "Word of mouth is new ads message," *Financial Times,* 18 June 2006.

4. Rob Walker, "The Hidden (in Plain Sight) Persuaders," *The New York Times,* 5 December 2004.

5. Ibid.

6. Ibid.

7. Robert Berner, "I Sold It Through the Grapevine," *BusinessWeek,* 29 May 2006.

8. Ibid.

CHAPTER 9 • The Fence Mender

1. Gallup Poll, "Honesty/Ethics in Professions," 14 December 2006.

2. Andrew Hampp, "At CTAM: Ogilvy's Steve Hayden Wants to Coin a New Acronym," *Advertising Age,* 25 July 2007.

3. Mya Frazier, "Ads to Be Printed on Grocery Store Conveyor Belts," *Advertising Age,* 16 August 2006.

4. Andrew Hampp, "A Taste of 'Rome,'" *Advertising Age,* 4 January 2007.

5. Alice Z. Cuneo, "That's Right: You Can Sponsor the Golden Gate Bridge," *Advertising Age,* 20 November 2006.

6. Lynn Upshaw, "Integrity in Marketing Is Not Optional," *Advertising Age,* 30 July 2007.

7. Seth Stevenson, "Head Case: The Mesmerizing Ad for Headache Gel," *Slate,* 24 July 2006.

8. Mya Frazier, "This Ad Will Give You a Headache, but It Sells," *Advertising Age,* 24 September 2007.

9. Yankelovich Partners, "Consumer Resistance to Marketing Reaches an All-Time High," 15 April 2004.

10. Ibid.

11. Matthew Creamer, "Just Make It Stop: 4A's Hires PR Help," *Advertising Age,* 25 September 2006.

12. Cone, Inc., "Multi-Year Study Finds 21% Increase in Americans Who Say Corporate Support of Social Issues Is Important in Building Trust," 8 December 2004.

13. Jessica Burnett, "The Rage Over (Red)," *Newsweek,* 14 March 2007.

14. Daniel Gross, "Oil Slicks," *Slate*, 15 October 2002.

15. Barbara Ehrenreich, "Welcome to Cancerland: A Mammogram Leads to a Cult of Pink Kitsch," *Harper's* magazine, November 2001.

16. Stephanie Thompson, "Breast Cancer Awareness Strategy Increases Sales of Campbell's Soup," *Advertising Age*, 3 October 2006.

17. Holly Buchanan, "Cause Marketing: Campbell's Soup," http://marketingto-womenonline.typepad.com/blog/2006/10/cause_marketing.html.

18. Blythe Bernhard, "When Pink Goes Inc.," the *Orange County Register*, 5 October 2006.

19. Harris Poll, "A very convenient truth," 5 July 2006.

20. Mya Frazier, "Costly Red campaign reaps meager $18M," *Advertising Age*, 5 March 2007.

Acknowledgments

I am extremely fortunate to be part of an amazing family full of people who share my enthusiasm for this book and who have supported my creative pursuits throughout life. They sat through piano recitals, read my fourth-grade writing compositions, tasted my made-up recipes, and were forced to watch the variety shows I created when I was eight. I am especially grateful to my amazing parents for their endless support and appreciation for my writing since the time I was able to hold a crayon.

Throughout the past year, I've enjoyed gleeful moments of downtime with the help of my sister, Joy; my parents, Don and Marina; and all of my great girlfriends. Thank you for the dinners, emails, and long phone conversations. Special thanks to Stacey Vanek-Smith and Amy Winn for reading the manuscript and lending me inspiration, advice, and humor.

Thanks to reporter Lisa Napoli, whose encouragement led me to produce what would become a very important radio story. I am also grateful to editor Jill Rothenberg for hearing that story on public radio and approaching me with the idea to write this book.

I've been so lucky to work with the wonderful people at Seal Press, especially my editor, Anne Connolly, who was my sounding board and shrink throughout the writing process, as well as Laura Mazer and Krista Lyons-Gould. Thanks to Mark Gordon, who's my agent at ICM but, more important, is a great friend.

Thank you to Microsoft for creating Microsoft Word, with its invaluable thesaurus and word-count tools. I used them nearly every day. Thank you to the wonderful baristas at Starbucks on Lake Avenue for refueling me with venti nonfat lattes and providing me with a friendly place to work when I got tired of my home office (and no, this is not a paid mention).

I am forever grateful to the many women across the country who answered my endless questions and revealed their insights, opinions, and personal stories.

Over the years, my writing has been shaped by many brilliant journalists. My thanks go out to the tremendous staff at American Public Media's "Marketplace." Thanks to my college professors who went beyond the call of duty in the early years, especially Eric Bishop, Mike Laponis, Don Pollock, George Keeler, and Shane Rodrigues. And I must thank three incredible women who have been amazing mentors to me: Liza Tucker, Judy Muller, and Sandra Thomas. I can never thank you enough for your caring support, patience, and wisdom.

Most important, I thank my husband, Nick Bernstein, who won my heart in less than thirty seconds and continues to bring joy, humor, love, and encouragement to me every day. I am one lucky girl.